Akhmatova's
Petersburg

Akhmatova in Tsarskoe Selo, ca. 1916

Akhmatova's Petersburg

Sharon Leiter

University of Pennsylvania Press
Philadelphia 1983

For my parents,
Selma and Al Sherman,
with love and gratitude

Credits

Cover and photo on p. 83 are from Leningrad: History, Art, and Architecture *by*
Nigel Gosling. Copyright © 1965 by E. P. Dutton & Co. Photos by Colin Jones.
Used with permission of Macmillan Publishing Co., Inc., acting as agent for
Crowell Collier Publishers Ltd., formerly part of Cassell Ltd. Studio Vista Ltd.
The following photos of Akhmatova on pp. ii, 12, and 144 are from Anna
Akhmatova, stikhi, perepiska, vospominanija, ikonografia, *compiled by Carl*
Proffer (Ann Arbor, Michigan: Ardis, 1977), and are used with permission.
The translation of Poem Without a Hero *by Carl Proffer with Assya Humesky*
from Anna Akhmatova *(Ann Arbor, Michigan: Ardis, 1977) is used with*
permission.
Other illustrative material from Russian publications.

This work was published with the support of the Haney Foundation.

Library of Congress Cataloging in Publication Data

Leiter, Sharon.
  Akhmatova's Petersburg.

  Bibliography: p.
  Includes index.
    1. Akhmatova, Anna Andreevna, 1889–1966—Criticism
and interpretation.   2. Leningrad (R.S.F.S.R.) in
literature.   I. Title.   II. Title: Petersburg.
PG3476.A324Z74   1983   891.71′42   82-40491
ISBN 0-8122-7864-X

Printed in the United States of America

Contents

Photographs

Preface

This book examines the work of one of Russia's greatest twentieth-century poets in light of its evolving vision of the city of Petersburg-Leningrad. Of those transitional writers who came of age in imperial Petersburg and survived into the Leningrad era, Anna Akhmatova was most consistently preoccupied with the Petersburg tradition and the possibilities for its survival in the Soviet world. The half century of her poetic landscape is dominated by the outline of her city, constant in its many incarnations. Inheriting the dark-hued, "unreal" city of Pushkin, Gogol, Dostoevsky, and Blok, Akhmatova was to adapt and transform the Petersburg myth through her unique vision: as a woman and as a refugee from the nineteenth to what she would call, "not the calendar, but the True Twentieth Century."

While this study primarily addresses specialists in Russian literature, I have also tried to speak to readers who have become acquainted with Akhmatova's poetry through English translations. I have therefore given all titles in both Russian and English, have rendered excerpts of Russian criticism and prose in English (translations are mine unless otherwise noted), and have provided a literal English version after each quotation of Akhmatova's verse. I use the transliteration systems of J. Thomas Shaw, *The Transliteration of Modern Russian for English-Language Publications* (Madison: University of Wisconsin Press, 1967). System I, which facilitates correct pronunciation by the reader unfamiliar with the Russian language, has been used for all proper and place names in the text, notes, bibliography, and index; System II, the Library of Congress system without diacritics, has been used for titles in notes and bibliography and, in the text, for words treated as words and for the titles of poems.

Generous support by the University of Virginia, which awarded me a sesquicentennial associateship and a faculty summer fellowship, enabled me to bring this work to completion. I wish to thank Elliott Mossman, Donald Fanger, and Sidney Monas, who read the manuscript and offered many valuable suggestions. I am deeply grateful to my friends and colleagues Gabor Follinus, Uliana Gabara, and Gloria Russo, whose wisdom and advice were always available to me. Among the friends whose support was essential to me during the writing of this book, I must single out for special gratitude my husband, Darryl Leiter. As always, I found his faith and encouragement indispensable. Finally, I would like to thank my daughter, Robin, for her love and patience during the difficult months.

Introduction

*My whole life has been connected with Leningrad;
in Leningrad I became a poet and Leningrad inspired
and coloured my poetry.*
  —Anna Akhmatova

*In general all of Leningrad, with all its squares, canals,
rivers, is so closely linked in my memory with the
poetry of Akhmatova, that for me, as for many readers,
Leningrad is inseparable from her.*
  —Korney Chukovsky

*T*he history of a poet and his city is always one of mutual shaping and transformation. "Granite is softer than wax," Akhmatova wrote in her later years, suggesting the city's malleability in time's hands as well as in the artist's; but granite is also a hard, stubborn substance, imposing its textures and contours upon the artist's imagination and forming his world view. When, as in the case of Petersburg, the city possesses, along with its stones and waters, a long and brilliant literary legend, its generative powers are multiplied several fold. Such a place continually gives birth to new visions of itself.

The multiplicity of Akhmatova's visions of Petersburg stems directly from its singular, enduring role in her life. Petersburg-Leningrad was, in her own words, the one city on earth she knew, the one to which she could grope her way even in sleep.[1] Although she was born on the Black Sea coast, Petersburg was her native city in every other sense of the term.[2] It was in turn-of-the-century Petersburg that she spent the formative years of youth (she was born in 1889), developed lifelong friendships, and came of age as a poet. She once wrote:

Был блаженной моей колыбелью
Темный город у грозной реки

The dark city on the terrible river
Was my blessed cradle

She called the city her cradle and her marriage bed and designated it the locus of her posthumous monument. And just as "the northern capital" was inextricable from the transformational moments of Akhmatova's life cycle, so she was witness to and participant in its own extraordinary twentieth-century history. She was present when imperial Petersburg became wartime Petrograd and when, in 1924, the city of the Bolshevik Revolution became Leningrad. During the Civil War and throughout the 1920s when the entrenchment of the new regime paralleled her own gradual exclusion from the official literary world, she lived in Leningrad. During the 1930s, while her contemporaries were banished or killed, Akhmatova's fate was "exile" within her one city. She was there when the Second World War broke out; and although she was evacuated to Tashkent during the siege, she returned to postblockade Leningrad in 1944 to mourn the enormity of the city's martyrdom. It was in this postwar necropolis that she, like other Russians, awaited liberalization and experienced the disappointment of this hope in her own condemnation to ten more years of literary exclusion following Zhdanov's indictment of her as "half-nun, half-whore."[3] The wavering "de-Stalinization" of Soviet cultural life, which ended decisively (a year after her death) with the 1967 trial of Sinyavsky and Daniel, was the final phase of Leningrad's history that she was to share. Most of her life had passed within the precincts of the city. Her trips to Europe in 1910 and 1912 as the young wife of Nikolay Gumilyov, and in 1965 as the elderly, honored poet of international stature, appear as deceptively bright prologue and ironic afterword to the confined Leningrad-centered text of her life.

Yet, while residing within her "one city" Akhmatova had lived in many. She wrote of this paradox in the fifties in her notes for an unfinished autobiographical book, in which a major section was to be devoted to Petersburg-Leningrad: "After Petersburg as I found it (at that time I was only an observer in the full sense of the word), I will say a few words about Petersburg of the teens, about war-time Petersburg, about revolutionary Petrograd. About the unforgettable (but for some reason wholly forgotten) year of 1919 and finally, about post-blockade Leningrad. So many layers!!!"[4] Akhmatova was to realize only a fraction of her plan for a historical prose chronicle of the city's incarnations, and one must look to her poetry for the many layers of her visions. In its journey through the "True Twentieth Century," Akhmatova's Petersburg became a protean expression of the poet's shifting model of the world, an intersection of personal and public, lyrical and legendary domains.

Like all writers of Russia's Silver Age, Akhmatova could not address herself to the subject of Petersburg without also taking into account its highly elaborated literary myth. So great was the impact of Peter's city on Russia's finest poetic imaginations that, by the turn of the century, the northern capital, so often evoked in terms of mists and shadows, now had a constant shadow companion: its literary double.[5]

Throughout the two hundred years of the "Petersburg period" of Russian history, the city's image was to fluctuate with the political and philosophical currents of the day. Eighteenth-century evocations, primarily in celebratory odes, had been wholly positive, praising the city as an unmitigated triumph of Reason and Russia over nature's intractability, a proud achievement of the Empire. Yet from the beginning, this very triumph was regarded by some as a fatal error. In the early nineteenth century, poet and historian Nikolay Karamzin gave voice to the notion that the place was cursed:

> Shall we close our eyes to yet another glaring mistake of Peter the Great? I mean his founding a new capital on the northern frontier of the state, amidst muddy billows, in places condemned by nature to barrenness and want. . . . the idea of establishing there the residence of our sovereigns was, is and will remain a *pernicious* one. How many people perished, how much money and labor was expended to carry out this intent? Truly, Petersburg is founded on *tears and corpses*.[6]

In the work of Pushkin, whom Antsiferov has called "in the same measure the creator of the *image* of Petersburg as Peter the Great was the builder of the city itself,"[7] the triumphant and the accursed cities were to stand side by side, implacably confronting one another. In his *Mednyi vsadnik* (*The Bronze Horseman*), the fate of the insignificant clerk Evgeny—whose betrothed drowns in one of the periodic floods which menace this city built, in defiance of nature, on the inhospitable Finnish swamps—poses an existential counterpoint to the ambitions of the emperor. An enduring ambivalence is introduced: for the dazzling and graceful city beloved by the narrator is also a metaphysical landscape whose vast granite expanses and seething waters threaten simultaneously to overwhelm both human significance and sanity.[8]

From Pushkin onward, the Petersburg cityscape, centering around the Neva, would embody the image of a Cosmos never wholly safe from the incursions of that Chaos from which it was wrested, a sense of the precariousness of human existence in the face of overwhelming historical and natural forces. In his "Petersburg Tale" Pushkin created the vision of the "fateful city" threatened by that hubris which is the price of overstepping the limits set for man, a city which must exist in eternal expectation of the Deluge.[9]

In Pushkin, too, the notion of unique Petersburg types and a distinctive quality of life rooted in the conditions of the city's founding and existence first enters literature. The premeditated creation of the city,[10] through Peter's will to carve for himself a "window on the West" overshadowing the old capital of Moscow and steering the country away from its cultural and religious traditions, led to the notion that the city's life had a rootless, unreal quality.[11] This concept found expression in the atmosphere and supernatural events of Pushkin's "Pikovaia dama" ("Queen of Spades"), which contained the seeds of the subsequent rich flowering of a "fantastic city," where the supernatural arises from the very midst of the mundane, where the evidence of the senses is an elaborate deception, and where delirium reigns, wrapping its victims in both ecstasy and horror before ultimately destroying them. Donald Fanger relates the emergence of this central aspect of the Petersburg myth to "the fact" of "the fantastic atmosphere of the city," "the peculiar Petersburg situation and climate,"[12] while Clarence Brown remarks that "the immense perspectives of Petersburg make it God's own setting for surrealism."[13] Whatever its roots in Petersburg's history, climate, and architectural plan, the fantastic city soon acquired an independent artistic life of its own in Gogol's "Peterburgskie povesti" ("Petersburg Tales"), where "the interpenetration of the real and the phantom, the probable and the improbable, the exalted and mundane, the tragic and the comic," are "projected upon the various levels of [the city's] life."[14] In Gogol, the supernatural is an expression of a soulless marionette world manipulated by an ironic, sinister puppeteer. In this city of illusion, where "the devil himself lights all the street lamps to show everything in anything but its true colors" ("Nevsky Prospect"), artists are destroyed by the pursuit of elusive purity and beauty or lose their souls to the spell of an evil portrait with living eyes; the outraged ghost of a downtrodden civil servant returns to take revenge for the theft of the overcoat, which had been the man's dearest possession, and the nose of another petty bureaucrat abandons its rightful facial position and goes off to live its own life, rising in social station above its original owner.

In Dostoevsky's development of this "double" theme, in his early novel of that name (*Dvoinik*), he goes beyond Gogol's joke, making the two civil servants, both named Golyadkin, into the opposite poles of a divided self. Petersburg's frozen streets and bridges, its relentless snow, sleet, and cold, are inseparable from the hero's mounting torments as he pursues his worthless double through the hostile capital; they are the landscape and climate of his exclusion from his own life. The distance between Gogol's fantastic city and Dostoevsky's city of delirium is thus a psychological one. As Fanger has shown in his major study of Dostoevsky's city: "The supernatural is banished and if its semblance at times seems to remain, it remains as the perception of real people, not marionettes. As a result, the city becomes really fantastic in its action on the people who live in it."[15] Fanger demonstrates how, throughout the many phases of its development, Dostoevsky's "most abstract and intentional city," sprung from the mind and will of the dictator, remains a city of the mind: the nightmare Petersburg of the dreamer, in which fantasy replaces life; the unnatural "anticity" of the "antihero," divorced from life, in *Zapiski iz podpol'ia* (*Notes from the Underground*). In his greatest Petersburg work, *Prestuplenie i nakazanie* (*Crime and Punishment*), the city is an expression of modern man's estrangement from the natural sources of his moral being:

. . . [Dostoevsky] presented for the first time the life of the city in all its sordidness—not simply to show what these conditions automatically did to people, as the naturalists would show, but to raise the problem of how, within them, sentient beings might pursue the quest for dignity. And on a less literal level, he raised the chaotic city to the position of a symbol of the chaotic moral world of man, so that the contradictions of the second find their counterpart in the contrasts of the first. He showed without abstraction bare human consciousness striving in a world where there were few of the usual categories of normality, striving with a terrible and unsought freedom, isolated and rootless, together without community, to rediscover the conditions of "living life." The nature of the struggle is ultimately intellectual, the seductions ideological, the goal a new or an old morality—something to fill the void.[16]

Victor Shklovsky's observations on the issue of literary borrowings are particularly relevant to the question of Akhmatova's indebtedness to this tradition in the creation of her own Petersburg. "Books are not the world, but windows on the world. The windows of various houses can open a view on one and the same landscape; this landscape is one and the same although it is variously seen. The likeness of the landscapes, at the same time, is not a borrowing from one window by another."[17]

In spite of the alterations of time from Pushkin's era to her own, the essential stability of Petersburg's outline, its architectural plan, the disposition of river and surrounding buildings and monuments, its natural and imperial bureaucratic climates, allowed Akhmatova to see the "same landscape" outside her window that her great predecessors had seen outside theirs. At the same time, from her earliest years, their city visions were her own treasured possessions. Pushkin's and Dostoevsky's Petersburgs were so much a part of the cultural heritage she shared with her ideal reader that she felt free to use a literary shorthand to suggest the essence of their city-worlds: the statue of Pushkin's *Bronze Horseman*, whose horse "freezes in terrible impatience," appears at the outset of the important early Petersburg poem "Stikhi o Peterburge" ("Verses about Petersburg"), while the words "Dostoevsky's Russia" open the great later Leningrad cycle "Severnie elegii" ("The Northern Elegies"). But these and numerous other image-reminiscences gleam like burnished fragments in a city mosaic which is uniquely her own.

Writing in the first years of the Soviet era, Antsiferov conceptualized the city's literary tradition as a finely regulated tension between continuity and innovation:

> The reflection of Petersburg in the souls of our verbal artists is not random; here one does not find the creative license of boldly expressed individualities. Behind all these impressions, one senses a definite consistency, one might say, a harmony. An inalterable impression is created that the soul of the city has its own fate and our writers, each in his own time, have marked a definite moment in the history of the development of the city's soul.[18]

Ultimately, it was Akhmatova's task to bring the nineteenth-century city into the twentieth. If her Petersburg "moment" spanned the chasm between the city's death and its Soviet afterlife, nonetheless she continued to claim for it, until her death in 1966, its central, symbolic role in Russian destiny. In this she was the last great poet of the Petersburg tradition.[19]

Notes

1. The lines are from the "Third Northern Elegy":

О, сколько очертаний городов
Из глаз моих могли бы вызвать слезы,
А я один на свете город знаю
И ощупью его во сне найду...

Oh, how many cities' outlines
Might have brought tears to my eyes,
But there is just one city on earth I know
And could grope my way to in sleep . . .
[I/311]

Bracketed volume and page numbers in the text refer to the two-volume Russian edition, *Anna Akhmatova: Sochineniia,* ed. G. P. Struve and Boris Filippov vol. 1, 2d ed., vol. 2 (Munich and Washington, D.C.: Inter-Language Literary Associates, 1967–68).

2. For the fullest available biography of the poet, see Amanda Haight, *Anna Akhmatova: A Poetic Pilgrimage* (New York and London: Oxford University Press, 1976).

3. See Haight, *Akhmatova,* pp. 143–47, for a complete account of the speech of Andrey Zhdanov.

4. This material, located in Akhmatova's archive in the Saltykov-Shchedrin Public Library in Leningrad, is described in the article "Nenapisannaia kniga" ("An Unfinished Book") by L. A. Mandrykina, in *Knigi, arkhivy, avtografy (Books, Archives, Autographs* (Moscow, 1973).

5. The extent to which the city had become a major nineteenth-century theme is apparent from the large number of authors treated in N. P. Antsiferov's *Dusha Peterburga (The Soul of Petersburg)* (Petersburg, 1922). Continuation of this trend in twentieth-century literature is documented in K. A. Afanasev, V. V. Zakharov, and B. V. Tomashevsky, comps., *Peterburg, Petrograd, Leningrad v russkoi poezii (Petersburg, Petrograd, Leningrad in Russian Poetry)* (Leningrad, 1975).

6. Richard Pipes, trans. and ed., *Karamzin's Memoirs on Ancient and Modern Russia* (New York: Atheneum, 1966), p. 126.

7. Antsiferov, *Dusha Peterburga,* p. 62.

8. For a full treatment of this subject, see B. V. Tomashevsky, ed., *Pushkinskii Peterburg (Pushkin's Petersburg)* (Leningrad, 1949).

9. See Antsiferov, *Byl'i mif Peterburga (Fact and Myth of Petersburg)* (Petersburg, 1924), pp. 61–64, for an analysis of Pushkin's *poema* with respect to the mythical significance of floods.

10. "Legend states: 'On the 16th of May 1703, Peter held two pieces of sod cross-wise and said, "A city shall exist here." Above him in the air an eagle soared.' Here is an interesting feature: before us is the city founder as he was conceived by ancient religion. Invol-

untarily one thinks of Romulus at the moment of the founding of Rome on the Palatine Hill when twelve hawks soared above his head" (Antsiferov, *Byl'i mif*, p. 28).

11. The rivalry of Petersburg and Moscow is as old as the new capital itself. Partisans on both sides long recognized a divergence in the life-styles of both cities so great that it set them apart as two separate cultures. In the nineteenth-century debate between Slavophiles and Westerners, the opposing essays of Herzen ("Moscow and Petersburg," 1842, in *Sobranie sochinenii* [*Collected Works*] [Moscow, 1934], 2:33–42) and Belinsky ("Petersburg and Moscow," 1845, in *Sobranie sochinenii* [*Collected Works*] [Moscow, 1948], 2:763–91) offered detailed sociological portraits of each city world, including its customs and their implications for Russia's future.

12. Donald Fanger, *Dostoevsky and Romantic Realism* (Cambridge, Mass.: Harvard University Press, 1965), pp. 105–106.

13. Clarence Brown, *The Prose of Osip Mandelstam* (Princeton, N.J.: Princeton University Press, 1965), pp. 35–36.

14. Fanger, *Dostoevsky*, p. 106.

15. Ibid., p. 165.

16. Ibid., p. 211.

17. Victor Shklovsky, *Za i protiv: Zametki o Dostoevskom* (*Pro and Contra: Notes on Dostoevsky*) (Moscow, 1957), p. 180.

18. Antsiferov, *Dusha Peterburga*, p. 39.

19. Only Akhmatova's great contemporary, friend, and fellow Petersburger Osip Mandelstam could compete for this title. But Mandelstam, who died in the camps in 1938, proclaimed the death of his beloved city shortly after the Revolution, and although he vowed eternal allegiance to the city as the home of poetry in his famous "V Peterburge my soidemsia snova" ("In Petersburg we will meet again"), he turned, in his poetry of the 1920s and 1930s, to Moscow as the locus of the new Soviet age. See my article: "Mandelštam's Moscow: Eclipse of the Holy City," *Russian Literature*, vol. 7, no. 2 (March 1980), pp. 167–97.

The Early Petersburg Love Poems

You are free, I am free,
Tomorrow is better than yesterday,—
Above the dark-watered Neva,
Beneath the cold smile
of Emperor Peter.
       —*Sochineniia*, I, 112

I

Akhmatova, 1924

The young Akhmatova, beginning her career in the imperial city, could hardly have suspected the culminating role she was to play in Petersburg's literary history. At that time, she seemed to be speaking, not a last word, but the first of a kind. From Gogol through Blok, the city streets had been haunted by the image of an elusive feminine ideal, incarnating the city's deceptive promise of salvation. In the "intimate diary" of Akhmatova's Petersburg lyrics, the feminine principle as passive, idealized object of the poet's quest was replaced by a supple, original feminine sensibility, itself seeking and defining the nature of fulfillment.

The outlines of Akhmatova's city first appeared shortly after Petersburg's literary image had been given a new direction by the city poetry of the French Symbolists, particularly Baudelaire and the Belgian poet Verhaeren. In this cultural importation, conducted largely through the self-conscious mediation of Valery Bryusov, Petersburg's traditional thematics were overlaid by those of the big city as modern man's new "element."[1] Wavering between Verhaeren's belief in a utopian city of the future and the Baudelairean vision of the terrifying face of the big city, Bryusov continually insisted upon the city as "the very essence of life."[2] The predominant pessimism of his city visions had the strongest influence upon the great poet of the city, Alexander Blok, whose first urban cycle, "Gorod" ("The City") (1904–1908), is connected by important thematic threads to Bryusov's *Urbi et Orbi* (*Cities and Worlds*) (1903). Blok's and Bryusov's apocalyptic visions of death within the context of the sordid, indifferent madness of the city[3] transformed "the city of delirium" into the language of fin-de-siècle malaise and mystical expectation. A spirit of decadence prevailed in the cabarets and restaurants of Blok's night city, abounding in "drunken streets" and "drunken crowds." Blok decried the spiritual chaos of the city in which all distinction between the sacred and the profane had been lost:

Здесь ресторан, как храмы, светел,
И храм открыт, как ресторан...

> *Here the restaurants, like temples, are lit up,*
> *And temples are open, like restaurants.*[4]

At the same time he sought, and momentarily found, his holy of holies in the midst of the profane:

> Ты право, пьяное чудовище!
> Я знаю: истина в вине.

> *You're right, drunken monster!*
> *I know: truth is in wine.*[5]

The image of the "Beautiful Lady"[6] ("Prekrasnaia dama") persistently intruded, suffusing the real with the mystical and infusing visions of the "blue lands" into the city's imprisoning perspectives. In the Blokian night world of tramps and demimondaines, with its intersection of the mystical and the everyday, Petersburg became the most perfect expression of the Silver Age's tormented quest for transcendence. From this Russian Symbolist city emerged both the Futurist city of the early Mayakovsky, with its despair and apocalyptic longing, and the Acmeist cities of Mandelstam—and Akhmatova.

In viewing Akhmatova's poetry against this tradition, critics have tended to stress the ways in which she differs from her Symbolist predecessors. In contrast with the "romantic distortion" and ephemerality of the Symbolists, Akhmatova's city has been described as "classically"[7] precise and concrete. The personal, affectionate, "proprietary" nature of her relationship to Petersburg has been juxtaposed with the Symbolists' estranged, historically pessimistic stance.[8] This emphasis has led at least one critic to deny that the city is an independent theme in Akhmatova's early poetry; Sam Driver sees it "not as a focus, but as a background for the love motif, as a backdrop for the drama."[9] As Zhirmunsky has noted, however, it is not possible to speak of scenic background in Akhmatova, in the true sense of the term: "She does not create an entire scenic picture, against which the action develops. With great sharpness of individual perception, she fixes separate impressionistic features, which are associated for her with the action, very often (following I. Annensky's example) with a sharp rupture between the landscape and the personal experience corresponding to it."[10] If Zhirmunsky's observation is correct, as I believe it is, then the mechanistic concept of action and background must be replaced with a more holistic one.[11] Akhmatova's Petersburg is never mere passive ornament or backdrop but rather constitutes a dynamic element in her transformation of the particulars of her life into the composite legend of a Petersburg "heroine" which emerges from the mosaic of individual poems.

From this point of view, the notion that Akhmatova's cityscapes show a realistic "precision" becomes questionable or at best irrelevant. The artistic significance of her Petersburg depends, not on the accuracy of her observations, but on the figurative uses to which they have been put. Like the city of the Symbolists, Akhmatova's Petersburg is the product of that process of metaphoric transformation which Weimar,[12] in his study of American fiction, has found to be central to the creation of fictional/poetic cities.

Spatial/Emotional Domains

In the early love poetry, city imagery functions as an emotional map, defining boundaries, designating sacred and nonsacred places. A momentary glimpse of narrow canals (I/65) and the "twilight gloom" of a white night (I/77) are all we find of Petersburg in Akhmatova's first book, Vecher (Evening, 1912). When the city's outline emerges in Chëtki (Rosary, 1914) and even more prominently in Belaia staia (White Flock, first edition, 1917), it is perceived in terms of spatial dichotomies which separate the heroine from her beloved and the realm of love from that of nonlove.

Spatial dichotomies can be clearly observed in two poems of 1913 in which the city appears as the uninviting outer place with respect to the warm, mysterious kingdom of the

lover, or potential lover. In "Zdravstvui! Legkii shelest sly-
shish'" ("Hello! Do you hear a light rustling," I/109), the
speaker, having come unbidden to interrupt her beloved's
writing, begs not to be chased from his house, where "it is
bright and simple," to the outside world

> Где под душным сводом моста
> Стынет грязная вода.

> *where under the stifling arch of the bridge*
> *The dirty water freezes.*

—a possible allusion to suicide.

In "O tebe vspominaiu ia redko" ("I remember you
rarely," I/122), the contrast of "his" domain and the external
city is contained in the image of "your red house above the
turbid river," which the heroine passes "on purpose," as she
foresees an "inevitable second meeting" with him. In their
brief appearance in these poems, the city's waters, presented
in their traditional negative coloration (cold, dirty, turbulent),
represent the realm of nonlove. The heroine is herself identi-
fied with the external, turbulent city; she is Akhmatova's
"witch" persona, who comes, in the first poem, as a disrup-
tive, semidisembodied spirit, and in the second, who "se-
cretly practices witchcraft on the future" and "bitterly dis-
turbs your sun-permeated peace." The poems are united by
the paradigm—a bright, simple, peaceful realm, to which the
heroine seeks entry, and a cold, turbulent one, to which she
belongs.

Sometimes the lover's realm is the city as a whole, envi-
sioned from the vantage point of the heroine's "exile" outside
the city. In "Pokorno mne voobrazhenie" ("Imagination obeys
me," I/105, 1913), two lines

> Прекрасных рук счастливый пленник
> На левом берегу Невы,

A happy prisoner of beautiful arms
On the left bank of the Neva,

establish Petersburg as someone else's paradise, where her former lover ("my renowned contemporary") enjoys another. The impossibility of mutually reciprocated love: "I love, but I am not loved. I am loved, but I do not love"—which Chukovsky [13] called the "constant theme" of the early Akhmatova—finds expression in images of geographical isolation. Outside Petersburg, in her "Tver solitude," she bitterly remembers him.

In "Kogda v mrachneishei iz stolits" ("When, in the gloomiest of capitals," I/158, 1916), exile from the city of love is voluntary, and the relationship viewed in retrospect is her own. The heroine has fled Petersburg; from the place of her refuge, presumably Pesochnaya Bukhta, where the poem was written, she recalls the day of her flight. The poem apparently alludes to Akhmatova's relationship with the artist Boris Anrep who, upon his return from Europe to take part in the war, came to see Akhmatova in April 1916 and brought her an altar cross he had found in a ruined church. Akhmatova's departure for the south at the end of the summer (she took the cross with her) was motivated by health considerations. [14] In the poem, however, the departure is transformed into an act of renunciation, and the gift of the cross becomes a hint of the perversity of the relationship, for it is given "on the day of betrayal."

The city's role in this poem is essential in creating the internal significance of the heroine's renunciation and flight, which are described only in terms of external events and images, that is, it serves as "objective correlative" [15] for the speaker's feelings. The poet begins by placing the action "in the gloomiest of capitals." This designation does more than identify the city as Petersburg, which is accomplished, in any case, by the later reference to the Neva; it establishes a connection between the speaker's personal drama and the "dark"

Petersburg tradition. Akhmatova asks the reader to regard this drama as conditioned by the city's dark essence, while at the same time she localizes the "gloom" within Petersburg. For the poem's argument, at least superficially, is that things are better, now that the heroine has left the city and has come to the "other place."

The initial movements of the inner drama are expressed in terms of a subtle tension between the speaker and images presented by the city. The "gloominess" of the capital is transmuted into a more positive plane in the image of the speaker writing her renunciation, with firm but tired hand on the "pure whiteness" of the page. The notions of calmness and purity inherent in these lines give way before the wind pouring through the round window, suggesting turbulence but also renewal, refreshment. Juxtaposed to this is the "passionate" dawn:

> Казалось, небо сожжено
> Червонно-дымною зарею.

> *It seemed the sky had been seared*
> *By a crimson-smoky dawn.*

And indeed, it is in the following stanza that the image of the lover is introduced.

Akhmatova approaches him through indirection, one might almost say through avoidance:

> Я не взглянула на Неву,
> На озаренные граниты,

> *I did not glance at the Neva,*
> *At the illuminated granite,*

These lines imply that it would be too dangerous, too painful to look. In an earlier poem, "Kak ty mozhesh' smotret' na Nevu?" ("How can you look at the Neva?" I/126, 1914),

Akhmatova suggests that the act of looking at the river is emotionally risky, inconceivable at certain moments, for it involves confronting the full reality of one's feelings and situation. In this poem, as in many others, the Neva and its granite embankments are associated with the love affair. As if to reinforce the avoidance of feeling inherent in this "not looking," the next two lines, in which the image of the beloved breaks through, are notably restrained:

И мне казалось — наяву
Тебя увижу, незабытый.

And it seemed to me—awake,
That I would see you, unforgotten one.

At this point, city images, rather than threatening to undo the speaker's restraint, cooperate in stifling her feelings and facilitating her flight:

Но неожиданная ночь
Покрыла город предосенний.
Чтоб бегству моему помочь,
Расплылись пепельные тени.

But an unexpected night
Covered the pre-autumn city.
To abet my flight,
Smoky shadows disintegrated.

Petersburg's unusual light collaborates in the transformation of still-living passion (the sky seared by a crimson-smoky dawn) into the burned-out half-life of "smoky shadows." [16]

In the poem's final stanzas, the speaker flees to the place which is "non-Petersburg," taking only the cross given her on the day of betrayal. There is a sense of minimalness and strain in this afterlife of love: only the cross on the empty wall preserves her from bitter, strange thoughts. Yet she is safe here from the feelings which threatened to overwhelm her in the city. Non-Petersburg is a neutral station, from which the past may be contemplated without terror:

> И ничего не страшно мне
> Припомнить, — даже день последний.

> *And nothing is terrible for me*
> *To remember—not even the last day.*

This same assertion of fearlessness associated with finding oneself outside Petersburg concludes another poem, "Kak ploshchadi eti obshirny" ("How vast these squares are," I/165–166, 1917). Here, too, Petersburg is the place of a love affair, from the intense recollection of which she awakens, in the poem's final lines, in her "country garden." The memory or dream of love is related wholly in the present tense, creating a sense of immediate experience.

> Как площади эти обширны,
> Как гулки и круты мосты!

> *How vast these squares are,*
> *How loud and steep the bridges!*

The squares and bridges of the city function as objective correlative; their extreme dimensions convey the "meaning" of the experience, which is less ecstatic than overwhelming: vast, steep, loud. In the next two lines,

> Тяжелый, беззвездный и мирный
> Над нами покров темноты.

> *Heavy, starless and peaceful*
> *Is the cover of darkness above us.*

positive (peaceful) and negative (heavy, starless) semantic

fields are merged.[17] The heavy darkness of the sky, which hides the lovers, is peaceful; the mood contrasts with the alarm of the previous two lines. Significantly, both this anxiety and heavy, starless peacefulness are positively invoked as the definition of the moment of love. The terms of love within the city are always extreme, difficult. Even in the second stanza, with its idyllic picture of the lovers "like mortals" walking "through the fresh snow," the miracle is that they are together for "the hour of parting."

In stanza 3, the sense of being overwhelmed, embodied in city images in stanza 1, is now expressed directly, in personal images of mounting passion, loss of control.

Безвольно слабеют колени,
И кажется, нечем дышать...

Falteringly my knees grow weak,
And it seems there's no air to breathe . . .

Akhmatova allows this mounting intensity to trail off in an ellipsis and then attempts to "counteract" it by replacing the narration of dynamic emotion with static definitions of his meaning to her:

Ты — солнце моих песнопений,
Ты — жизни моей благодать.

You are the sun of my solemn hymn-singing,
You are the godsend of my life.

When city imagery returns in the final stanza

Вот черные зданья качнутся,
И на землю я упаду, —

Now the black buildings will sway,
And I will fall to the earth,—

it takes the speaker simultaneously in two mutually opposed directions. For the swaying buildings, signifying the loss of a stable reality as she "falls," also signal the disintegration of the memory-dream and her return to the stability of the country garden. The very richness and intensity of her visions has fortified her against the terror of awakening alone, away from him:

> Теперь мне не страшно очнуться
> В моем деревенском саду.

> *Now I'm not afraid of awakening*
> *In my country garden.*

The dream structure of the poem encapsulates the love affair within a snowy, nocturnal Petersburg whose overwhelming physical qualities are both reflection and projection of the speaker's feelings. Like the "Tver solitude" of "Imagination obeys me" and the room with the cross on the empty wall of "When in the gloomiest of capitals," the country garden of this poem is not elaborated but merely designates a kind of bland, provincial afterlife following genuine, intense, and painful emotional experience whose locus is the city.[18]

This same paradigm recurs in a number of other poems where, however, no spatial designation is given to the afterlife; Petersburg, as the place of a past, lost love, is viewed from a nonlocalized present. "V poslednii raz my vstretilis' togda" ("For the last time we met then," I/115, 1914) evokes the lovers' last meeting on the banks of the Neva.[19] The river setting, which has played and will continue to play such a large role in the Petersburg love poems, functions as more than a stylized backdrop. As Vinogradov has observed,[20] the manner in which the threat of flood is mentioned gives it a special connection to the heroine's situation, establishing the singularity of that particular moment

Была в Неве высокая вода,

The waters of the Neva were high.

as well as an objectively perceived concern of the city as a whole:

И наводненья в городе боялись.

And in the city floods were feared.

Thus the tradition of the city as a place of natural disaster (the city of *The Bronze Horseman*) stands as objective correlative for the personal situation: approaching crisis, waters on the verge of overflowing their banks. The lover's reproach to the heroine is semantically related to the notion of "overflowing banks," for, he tells her, she has overstepped her proper limits as a woman:

Он говорил о лете и о том,
Что быть поэтом женщине — нелепость.

He spoke of summer and of the fact
That for a woman to be a poet is—an absurdity.

At this reproach the "water level" of her feelings rises, in an intense concentration on the surrounding architecture:

Как я запомнила высокий царский дом
И Петропавловскую крепость! —

How I memorized the tall, royal house
And the Peter and Paul fortress!—

The "tall, royal house" resonates with the "high water" of the Neva; but if "high water" is a symbol of instability, a "tall house" has the opposite connotation: stability, solidity. Linked to the adjective "royal," it forms a positively charged semantic unit. The second element of the memory, the Peter and Paul fortress, adds to the notion of high, impressive structures connotations of both impermeability and imprisonment. It is as if the heroine were attempting to appropriate these architectural qualities for her inner life as well as finding in them an objective correlative adequate to the significance of the moment.

In the "explanation" for the heroine's "memorization" given in the final stanza, there is neither high water nor tall, imprisoning buildings but instead the two free, dimensionless gifts of air and song:

Затем, что воздух был совсем не наш,
А как подарок Божий — так чудесен.
И в этот час была мне отдана
Последняя из всех безумных песен.

Because the air was not ours at all,
But like a gift of God—so marvelous.
And in that hour I was given back
The last of all the mad songs.

The return of the "last of all the mad songs" signifies both the end of the love affair—the rejection of her love—and the speaker's regaining of freedom as a poet from the lover who denied her right to be one.

In a Petersburg poem of the previous year, "O, eto byl prokhladnyi den'" ("Oh, it was a cool day" I/120, 1913), Akhmatova makes a similar assertion: her poetry will survive beyond the failure of love. Like the heroine of "For the last time we met then," who is rejected for the "absurdity" of being both woman and poet, the speaker of this poem has been rejected for her spiritual powers:

Пусть он не хочет глаз моих,
Пророческих и неизменных.

What if he does not want my eyes,
Prophetic and unchanging.

She asserts the inescapability of this power, as it manifests itself through her verse, paradoxically designated as "the prayer of my haughty lips." On one level, this is a Pyrrhic victory, for her connection with the beloved will not be a flesh-and-blood one. But Akhmatova, in prophesying her continued presence in his life, is affirming that the spiritual plane—her art—offers a form of survival in the face of "earthly" loss.

How does the city imagery of the first stanza function with respect to the affirmation contained in its second, last stanza?

О, это был прохладный день
В чудесном городе Петровом!
Лежал закат костром багровым,
И медленно густела тень.

Oh, it was a cool day
In Peter's marvelous city!
The sunset lay like a crimson bonfire,
And the shadow slowly thickened.

What is immediately striking is a strange disappointment of expectation when this city materializes. There is solemnity and intense emotion in the archaic diction of the poem's opening exclamation. But the marvelous city never appears. There is no architecture, neither the waters of the Neva nor its granite embankments—only weather and the play of light and shadow. The gaping "omission" between the exclamation point of line 2 and the twilight of lines 3 and 4 refocuses the

reader's eye from the "marvelous city" to the "cool day." Orig-
inally perceived in the context of the opening line's exaltation
as something bracing, the coolness of the day is now seen as a
stage before coldness, just as the glorious twilight of line 3
precedes the slowly thickening shadow of line 4. The mar-
velous city turns to shadow before we ever see it. If the stanza
as a whole is viewed, not only as an evocation of a memora-
ble, perhaps last, day of love within the city, but as objective
correlative for the internal drama, then the city imagery may
be seen as providing the counterstatement to the poem's final
affirmation. For if the thickening shadow as an image of the
insubstantial in the process of taking on substance parallels
the assertion of the endurance of the poet's verse (a parallel
reinforced on the euphonic level—"I *medlenno gu*stela *ten'*"
("And slowly the shadow thickened"), "*Molitvu gub m*oikh
nad*mennykh*" ("The prayer of my haughty lips")—within the
context of the first stanza it is also an image of loss; the trans-
formation of the cool day within the marvelous city into
shadow, half-life.

In "Stikhi o Peterburge" ("Verses about Petersburg,"
I/111, 1913), a far more elaborate network of city imagery
functions similarly in establishing an ambiguous attitude to-
ward questions of loss and survival. As the title indicates,
Petersburg itself is the subject of the poem, the central reality
in terms of which Akhmatova interprets the failure of the love
affair. Simply stated, the speaker finds consolation in the as-
sertion that her lost love will live on in the immortality of the
city. In Verheul's formulation: "The sense of the history of a
city or a nation as a timeless continuum—of which the living
quality of Peter's statue and the architectonic details of his city
serve as a symbol—is brought into relation with the sense of
a timeless extension of significant moments across the linear
differential of time in subjective experience." [21] Verheul notes
that the reader fails to take the speaker's happy expectation of
a new life at face value because it conflicts with the sense of
the future developed earlier in the poem, where "she imag-
ined the continuation of time as its *suspension*, an infinite ex-

pansion (navsegda . . . naveki) of the present moment, in which objects (neraskrytyi veer moi) and the architectonic details of the capital retain their reality, but in which personal existence is reduced to a reflected semi-life."[22] Yet the existence of two disparate visions of the future may not satisfactorily explain the hollowness of the poem's closing optimism. The fixed, unchanging future belongs to the love affair, the free, dynamic future to the mortal man and woman who survive that love. The consolation the speaker proposes is that their love has been part of the history of the city and as such will live on. She explicitly denies the need for "long years" of actual love, in favor of this spiritual alliance with the city. The "immortality" of their love is based upon the couple's having stood together during a "blessed moment of miracles:"

Оттого, что стали рядом
Мы в блаженный миг чудес,
В миг, когда над Летним садом
Месяц розовый воскрес, —

Because we stood side by side
At the blessed moment of miracles,
When above the Summer Garden,
The pink moon was resurrected,—

This notion of the city's "blessed repetitions" is present as well in the opening image of part 1:

Вновь Исакий в облаченьи
Из литого серебра.

Again St. Isaacs is
In vestments of cast silver.[23]

The sanctity and regularity of such fulfilled "public" expectations—the moon rising above the eternal city, the cloud "vestments" surrounding the dome of St. Isaac's (the Russian word for vestments, *oblachenie*, is built on the same root as the word for "cloud," *oblaka*)—is sharply contrasted with the tension and uncertainty in the expectation of "wearying meetings" at the private place, the "hateful window."

The failure of the poem to project convincingly a better future for the man and woman liberated from this tormenting love is to be found in the "undercutting" of the jingling trochaic rhythm in which the optimism is expressed. Above all, however, the description of the bounded space in which that future will take place betrays the bravado of the speaker's attempt to cover hidden pain:

> Ты свободен, я свободна,
> Завтра лучше, чем вчера, —
> Над Невою темноводной,
> Под улыбкою холодной
> Императора Петра.

> *You are free, I am free,*
> *Tomorrow is better than yesterday,—*
> *above the dark-watered Neva,*
> *beneath the cold smile*
> *of Emperor Peter.*

Indeed, the poem has developed two Petersburgs, or rather, two definitions of the city's "immovability." The first is that of a *positive immobility* associated with the permanence of architecture (St. Isaac's, the arch on Gallery Street), the recurrence of natural phenomena harmonized within the city's structures (the moon rising above the Summer Garden), and the spiritual survival of a love, which took place within the precincts of these lasting things. But the notion of a *negative immobility* is juxtaposed to this from the outset: the image of St. Isaac's is immediately followed by that of Peter's horse:

> Стынет в грозном нетерпеньи
> Конь Великого Петра.

In terrible impatience
The horse of Peter the Great freezes.

Here architecture's permanence is imprisoning. In contrast to the speaker's bestowal of ultimate value upon the city, the references to Peter interject a dissonant undertone. Following an image of the "stifling," "stern" wind sweeping soot down from black chimney pipes (in sharp counterpoint to the silvery immobility of St. Isaac's), the speaker exclaims:

Ах! своей столицей новой
Недоволен Государь.

Ah! the Sovereign is dissatisfied
With his new capital.

The cause of the sovereign's attitude is unclear, for the "pollution" may be read as accompaniment to, rather than as impetus for, his displeasure. When the image of the emperor occurs for the third time, framing the poem, the sense of a negative fatality is enhanced by the "darkness" of the Neva's waters and the "coldness" of the emperor's smile. Thus if Petersburg embodies a reassuring cultural continuity, it also stands for a negative, inescapable fate, a bounded, distinctly ominous stage on which the drama of the "free" man and woman must be enacted.

The Stern, Dark, Many-Watered City

This dark city, strongly associated with the dark waters of the Neva, predominates in the early love poetry, and Akhmatova paints it in varying emotional shades. Solemn acceptance of the stern conditions of Petersburg love is the sustained mood of "Bozhii Angel, zimnim utrom" ("God's Angel, on a winter morning," I/128, 1914). Akhmatova weaves city and love affair together through the pervasive notion of a "dark blessing." "Dark" and "light" meanings are wedded in every line of stanza 1:

Божий Ангел, зимним утром
Тайно обручивший нас,
С нашей жизни беспечальной
Глаз не сводит потемневших.

God's Angel, on a winter morning,
Having secretly betrothed us,
From our sorrowless life
Does not lift his darkened eyes.

—line 1: Angel/winter; line 2: betrothal/secretly; line 3: the use of the bookish word "bespechalnyi"—sorrowless, evokes the notion of sorrow, while negating it; line 4: the Angel's faithfully watching eyes are darkened. This dark blessing which defines the nature of their love, is then given as the reason for the couple's affection for the city and their meetings within it:

Оттого мы любим небо,
Тонкий воздух, свежий ветер
И чернеющие ветки
За оградою чугунной.

Оттого мы любим строгий,
Многоводный, темный город,
И разлуки наши любим,
И часы недолгих встреч.

That is why we love the sky,
The delicate air, fresh wind
And blackening branches
Behind the iron fence.

That is why we love the stern,
Many-watered and dark city,
And we love our partings
And the hours of our brief meetings.

The darkness of the angel's eyes is carried forward in the delicate, dynamic image of "blackening branches" and in the solid, static image of the "dark city." This is a winter love in a winter city (winter is, by far, the most characteristic Petersburg season in Akhmatova's love poems). The austerity of their "farewells" and "hours of brief meetings" is paralleled by the austerity of the city. What is striking is the perfect harmonization of city and love affair. Acceptance, and even love, of a stern but beautiful destiny associated with the city are elements of Akhmatova's Petersburg which will reappear in later poetry, in the context of the city's historical destiny.[24]

More often, however, in this early period, the angels hovering above her city are threatening rather than benevolent. More characteristic than the tranquillity of the preceding poem is anxiety associated with a powerful sense of sin, guilt, and impending retribution. In the three-line "Prostish' li mne eti noiabr'skie dni?" ("Will you forgive me these November days?" I/111, 1913), the "Japanese" poem,[25] in which all is left unsaid—the meaning of the "tragic autumn," the reason the speaker must be forgiven—the single visual image of the lights "shattering" in the Neva canals is made to bear the weight of these tragic connotations:

Простишь ли мне эти ноябрьские дни?
В каналах приневских дробятся огни.
Трагической осени скудны убранства.

Will you forgive me these November days?
In the Neva canals lights shatter.
The attire of tragic autumn is meager.

The ability of Neva imagery to sustain this unexplicated symbolic burden seems to be taken for granted by the poet, on several occasions. Mention has already been made of "How can you look at the Neva?" (I/126, 1914), in which the reader is not directly told why it seems so extraordinary to the speaker that the addressee is capable of looking at the Neva or walking onto its bridges:

Как ты можешь смотреть на Неву,
Как ты можешь всходить на мосты?..
Я недаром печальной слыву
С той поры, как привиделся ты.
Черных ангелов крылья остры,
Скоро будет последний суд,
И малиновые костры,
Словно розы, в снегу цветут.

How can you look at the Neva,
How can you walk up onto the bridges? . . .
Not in vain am I said to be sad
Since the time when I first dreamed of you.
The wings of black angels are sharp,
The last judgment will soon come,
And crimson bonfires,
Like roses, blossom in the snow.

In this poem, lacking all explanatory transitions, the related notions of passion, sadness, sin, and retribution reflect back upon the poem's opening questions, suggesting the cumulative reality, which the speaker cannot confront, incarnate in the river and its bridges.

Akhmatova's "night city" is dominated by these themes of sin and retribution. In her famous "My vse brazhniki zdes', bludnitsy" ("We're all drunkards here, harlots," I/97, 1913), her evocation of the dreary, insular nightclub world,[26] in which neither nature (on the walls the flowers and the birds, which pine for the clouds), nor human relations (the eyes of her lover resembling those of a cautious cat) are genuine, ends on a fearful prophetic note:

О, как сердце мое тоскует!
Не смертного ль часа жду?

А та, что сейчас танцует,
Непременно будет в аду.

Oh, how my heart aches!
Isn't it my last hour I'm awaiting?
And that woman who's dancing now
Will certainly go to hell.

The moral preoccupation of Akhmatova's night world is evident in a poem of the following year "Noch'iu" ("At Night," I/187, 1918), where the city is a static tableau against which the poet views the contrasting nights of the unfaithful and the faithful wife:

Стоит на небе месяц, чуть живой,
Средь облаков струящихся и мелких,
И у дворца угрюмый часовой
Глядит, сердясь, на башенные стрелки.

Идет домой неверная жена,
Ее лицо задумчиво и строго,
А верную в тугих объятьях сна
Сжигает негасимая тревога.

The moon stands in the sky, barely alive
Amid the small, streaming clouds,
And near the palace the gloomy guard
Looks angrily at the watch-tower clock.

An unfaithful wife walks home,
Her face is preoccupied and stern,
And unquenchable anxiety consumes the faithful wife
In the tight embraces of sleep.

In another poem, the heroine's guilt and remorse turn the Petersburg "Belaia noch'" ("White Night," I/340, 1914) into a dead, hellish landscape of retribution:

Небо бело страшной белизною,

А земля как уголь и гранит.

Под иссохшей этою луною

Ничего уже не заблестит.

The sky is white with a terrible whiteness,
But the earth is like coal and granite.
Beneath this dried-out moon
Nothing will ever shine.

The color white, often associated by Akhmatova with death, here is a color of terror. There is no movement in this lifeless city, and the only sound is that of a woman of the streets:

Женский голос, хриплый и задорный,

Не поет, кричит, кричит.

Надо мною близко тополь черный

Ни одним листком не шелестит.

A woman's voice, hoarse and provocative,
Doesn't sing, cries out, cries out.
Close above me, the black poplar
Doesn't rustle a single leaf.

If, in these poems, Akhmatova's city takes its place alongside Petersburg's numerous depictions, during those years, as the "sinful city"—Sodom or Babylon—on the verge of apocalypse, there is an essential difference. For Akhmatova, guilt resides in the erotic/personal lives lived within the city's confines. She never generalizes this perception historically to create in the reader a sense of the "accursed" nature of the city itself, the Slavophile view of Peter's tragically misguided venture, which so many writers of the Silver Age revived as a symbol of the impending destruction of Western (both European and Russian) culture.[27]

In some instances, the city itself, in its stern immovability, stands in judgment of the speaker and serves as an instrument of punishment. "Ne v lesu my, dovol'no aukat',—" ("We're not in the woods, stop hallooing,—" I/128, 1914) is another poem of guilty love, for the lover has "other cares, another wife." The speaker reproaches him for failing to come and soothe her wounded conscience and for abandoning her to the merciless Petersburg spring:

И глядит мне в глаза сухие
Петербургская весна.

Трудным кашлем, вечерним жаром
Наградит по заслугам, убьет.
На Неве под млеющим паром
Начинается ледоход.

And the Petersburg spring
Looks into my dry eyes.

With a heavy cough, with evening fever,
It will reward according to merit, will kill.
On the Neva, beneath fainting smoke,
The drifting of ice begins.

The heroine's eyes are dry: she does not weep for this love, whose spiritual aftermath must be inferred from the city imagery of the final stanza. It is likely that the reality of Akhmatova's tuberculosis, aggravated by the city's cold, damp climate, underlies the references to cough and fever. But Akhmatova transforms them into punishments to be inflicted by the harsh city/season. In the culminating image of the beginning ice drift, signifying both spring's renewal and the destruction of its floods, she suggests that powerful forces of mixed creative and destructive potential are about to be loosed.

If the fate of the abandoned heroine is uncertain in this poem, two other poems of the period project her wholly comfortless death within the city precincts. In "Kogda o gor'koi

gibeli moei" ("When of my bitter demise," I/178, 1917), the
city is once again the place of the love affair's significant mo-
ments. But the time perspective through which it is viewed is
complex: the speaker (in the present) imagines a time in the
future when her former lover will learn of her death. She
prophesies that, at that moment in the future, he will re-
member the Petersburg past. Typical of the Byronic lover of
Akhmatova's early poems, he will not grow "sterner or sad-
der" at the news of her death but will only "smile drily"—

> И сразу вспомнит зимний небосклон
> И вдоль Невы несущуюся вьюгу,
> И сразу вспомнит, как поклялся он
> Беречь свою восточную подругу.

> *And at once recall the winter sky*
> *And the snowstorm rushing along the Neva,*
> *And at once recall how he vowed*
> *To protect his Eastern girlfriend.*

The implication is that, while not grief stricken, he will at
least feel the recognition of his failure toward her. And the
Petersburg scene is the gateway to memory, the bearer of that
recognition of failed responsibility. In this remembered scene,
the figure of the heroine is absent; instead, the wintry image
of the Neva represents the full reality of their love, a use of
Neva imagery previously observed. The unexpected refer-
ence to herself as his "Eastern" girlfriend implies that he is a
foreigner, a West European, and that the distance between
them is, on one level at least, a geographical one. If Peters-
burg here is the representation of past love and failed prom-
ises, it is also the isolated "Eastern" place where the heroine's
death occurs, for he will hear of her death long after the fact:

> Когда о горькой гибели моей
> Весть поздняя его коснется слуха,

When of my bitter demise
Late news reaches his ears,

Although the poem is dated 1917, nothing in it specifically justifies a political interpretation of the heroine's sense of her impending death, which is related instead to love or to neglected love. The poem's central statement is the assertion of a minimal victory: he will not wholly escape the pain of her death.

Even this satisfaction is lacking from the image of martyrdom in "Ia s toboi, moi angel, ne lukavil" ("I didn't pretend with you, my angel," I/214, 1922). The speaker here is a man addressing the woman whom he has unwittingly destroyed:

Как же вышло, что тебя оставил
За себя заложницей в неволе
Всей земной непоправимой боли?

How did it happen that I left you
As a hostage, in place of myself,
In captivity to all earth's irreparable pain?

The Petersburg of this poem is the wintry, postrevolutionary city of cold and bonfires in the streets, a place of wind and stray bullets, which Akhmatova wrote about in her memoirs of Mandelstam:

Под мостами полыньи дымятся,
Над кострами искры золотятся,
Грузный ветер окаянно воет,

Under the bridges, unfrozen patches of river smoke,
Sparks flash golden above bonfires,
The heavy wind howls desperately.

But here, paradoxically, the random shooting becomes personalized as the woman's fate:

И шальная пуля за Невою
Ищет сердце бедное твое.

And a stray bullet beyond the Neva
Seeks your poor heart.

The Neva, consistently associated with the heroine's (pre-dominantly unhappy) love affairs, here is the place of her tragic death.

Yet in the poem's final lines, we see the heroine's martyr-dom, not outdoors near the river, but in an interior place, which is, however, as cold and comfortless as the external city:

И одна в дому оледенелом,
Белая лежишь в сияньи белом,
Славя имя горькое мое.

And alone in the icy house,
White you lie in a white radiance,
Praising my bitter name.

In her famous poem "Molitva" ("Prayer," I/152, 1915), Akhmatova willingly invoked the sacrificial role performed in the service of country. And in her later poetry, the theme of Petersburg-Leningrad's martyrs, those who remain within the city sharing its fate, takes on a principled, patriotic mean-ing. Here, although the heroine is a saintly figure ("my an-gel," "white, in a white radiance," "praising my bitter name"), the significance of her martyrdom is unclear. As in "When, of my bitter demise," her death is related to her abandonment within the city. Yet the man, who "did not pretend," does not himself understand how he came to play this destructive role. His perplexity, in conjunction with the phrase "hostage to all the earth's irreparable pain," as well as the images of the embattled city, creates a sense of a larger net of circum-stances entangling them both. The wholly bleak, comfortless

Petersburg of these poems is a place of death for the woman abandoned by her lover.

Arrivals

If, in Akhmatova's early portfolio, her city of love is most often drawn in varying gradations of darkness (albeit with white the color of death),[28] one also finds there rare, positive visions of Petersburg as the landscape of love's fulfillment.

The fateful association of the Neva with Akhmatova's lovers takes an unusual turn in "Pobeg" ("Flight," I/129, 1914). Ostensibly the poem depicts the flight of two lovers to a white yacht on the Neva. The man is the instigator of this adventure; the woman comes with reluctance, even terror, in a dreamlike state. And her emotions play a large role in establishing a symbolic level of meaning that underlies what is described.[29] The flight to the water is seen as a descent from the familiar world of the living to a dark underworld:

> Мимо зданий, где мы когда-то
> Танцовали, пили вино,
> Мимо белых колонн Сената
> Туда, где темно, темно.

> *Past buildings where once*
> *We danced, drank wine,*
> *Past the white columns of the Senate,*
> *To that place, where it's dark, dark.*

Akhmatova sustains the concrete reality of the adventure through specific detail (the sea rope that burns their nostrils, the person calling from a bridge), and the cheerfulness of the man's reply:

> «Что ты делаешь, ты безумный!» -
> «Нет, я только тебя люблю!
> Этот ветер — широкий и шумный,
> Будет весело кораблю!»

> *"What are you doing, you're mad!"* —
> *"No, it's just that I love you!*
> *This wind is sweeping and noisy,*
> *The ship will sport!"*

Yet she continually suggests another level of meaning:

> Горло тесно ужасом сжато,
> Нас в потемках принял челнок...

> *My throat constricted in terror,*
> *The barque received us in the shadows . . .*

When the dreamlike state, accompanied by the steady splashing of oars against the heavy Neva wave, is broken by the black sky's growing light and by someone calling to them from a bridge, the anxious heroine "with both hands" presses the chain of her cross to her breast and is carried, exhausted, to their final destination:

> Обессиленную, на руках ты,
> Словно девочку, внес меня,
> Чтоб на палубе белой яхты
> Встретить свет нетленного дня.

> *You carried me, exhausted,*
> *Like a little girl, in your arms,*
> *So that we might meet, on the deck of a white yacht,*
> *The light of the imperishable day.*

The whiteness of the yacht reestablishes the whiteness of the columns in the world left behind. The new day is called "imperishable," which, after the descent to the "underworld," suggests eternity. But the epithet "imperishable" also describes the quality of the time the lovers have seized for themselves. The flight to a haven *on the river itself* (in distinction from the number of times Akhmatova's lovers have met *near*, looked *at* the river, or refused to look at it) is a rare image of love's fulfillment, albeit not unaccompanied by great anxiety.[30]

Finally, two poems reverse the predominant pattern of partings and establish Petersburg as the place of first meeting. Heroine and city merge in passive expectation of the beloved, who enters their precincts from the outer place. The earlier poem "Dolgo shël cherez polia i sëla" ("He walked for a long time through fields and villages," I/143, 1915) focuses upon the journey of the hero, who wanders through the countryside seeking his beloved:

> «Где она, где свет веселый
> Серых звезд — ее очей?

> *Where is she, where is the gay light*
> *Of gray stars—her eyes?*

In contrast to the usual Petersburg winter, these are the "dimly flaming" last days of spring. The city is first defined as "our gloomy city" and is compared, in the hero's mind, with Venice and London, which enables the reader to recognize it immediately as Petersburg. In the following stanza, however, an unexpected transmigration of the city's familiar attributes occurs: both its darkness and its granite are woven into the image of a marvelous church and a moment of revelation:

> Стал у церкви темной и высокой
> На гранит блестящих ступеней
> И молил о наступленьи срока
> Встречи с первой радостью своей.

> А над смуглым золотом престола
> Разгорался Божий сад лучей:
> «Здесь она, здесь свет веселый
> Серых звезд — ее очей».

> *He stood near the dark, tall church*
> *On the granite of brilliant steps*

> *And prayed for the coming of that time*
> *Of meeting with his first happiness.*
>
> *And above the tawny gold of the throne*
> *There shone out God's garden of rays:*
> *"She is here, here is the gay light*
> *Of gray stars—her eyes."*

Petersburg is here the predestined city of fairy tales and legend where the hero finds his happiness.[31]

A sense of the miraculous is even stronger in the second, later poem of a first meeting, "Nebyvalaia osen' postroila kupol vysokii" ("A fantastic autumn built a tall cupola," I/224, 1922), but here the beloved appears only at the last moment, as the quiet, almost anticlimactic "conclusion" to the evocation of the fantastic season: not the naturally "dimly flaming" last days of spring, but an unnatural "springlike autumn." As in the previous poem, central to the city is an image of a holy place, represented here, however, not as man's architecture, but as nature's:

> Небывалая осень построила купол высокий,
> Был приказ облакам этот купол собой не темнить.
>
> *A fantastic autumn built a high cupola.*
> *There was an order to the clouds not to darken this cupola.*

Nature has grown purer, brighter, more beautiful. The waters of the murky canals have become emerald; nettles smell like roses, only more strongly. Akhmatova establishes the public nature of the miracle by the phrases: "and people were amazed" and "We all remembered them until the end of our days"—which locates the speaker in a time frame far distant from the events described (indeed, at the end of her—and her generation's—days) and enhances the legendary quality of the earlier time. Yet in the poem's final line, nature's entire performance is seen as prelude to the approach of a beloved, whose "calmness" is in stark contrast to all that has preceded it:

Вот когда подошел ты, спокойный, к крыльцу моему.

That was when you, calm, approached my porch.

This calmness contrasts with the violence, passion, and unbearable "devilish" intensity which have been part of the city's transformation:

Было душно от зорь, нестерпимых, бесовских и алых,
Их запомнили все мы до конца наших дней.
Было солнце таким, как вошедший в столицу

                 мятежник,

И весенняя осень так жадно ласкалась к нему,
Что казалось — сейчас забелеет прозрачный

                   подснежник...

It was stuffy from dawns, unbearable, devilish and crimson,
We all remembered them until the end of our days.
The sun was like a rebel entering

                 the capital,

And the spring-like autumn so hungrily caressed it
That it seemed the transparent snowdrop would instantly

                 grow white . . .

These sun-related images add a distinctly erotic content to the miraculous time: the violence of the sun, which is compared with a rebel entering the capital (the first "entrance" into the city), provokes the caresses of the springlike autumn, which bring about the climactic whitening of the snowdrop. This intense "arrival" is in stark contrast to the calm approach of the beloved. The ambivalence surrounding the word "calm" makes it possible to interpret the lover as the bearer either of a peaceful quality, signifying the positive fulfillment of all that has preceded him, or of that cold detachment so characteristic of Akhmatova's Byronic heroes. There is, in any case, a sense of the arbitrary nature of this line; one could imagine it replaced with a number of other variants. The core of the poem is a vision of the city (here a city of nature's architecture), whose "fantastic" life stirrings in a time of death (autumn) are both in themselves miraculous and precursory to the arrival of an even greater miracle. The peripheral role of the beloved indicates a redistribution of emphasis in the Petersburg poems of this period: emerging from its role in defining texture and contour in the topography of love, the city itself, as historical reality, now moves to the center of Akhmatova's poetic focus.

Notes

1. For an excellent discussion of this topic, see Georgette Donchin, *The Influence of French Symbolism on Russian Poetry* (The Hague: Mouton, 1958), pp. 151–63. Also see Korney Chukovsky, *Ot Chekhova do nashikh dnei* (*From Chekhov to Our Times*) (Ann Arbor: University Microfilms, 1968), for an account different from Donchin's regarding the emergence of the city theme in Russian poetry. Chukovsky assigns an important role to Konstantin Balmont. According to Lydia Chukovskaya's account, Akhmatova strongly associated the city theme with Chukovsky's writing: "'He was, after all, the first to proclaim that the city had entered poetry,' said Anna Andreevna," *Zapiski ob Anne Akhmatovoi* (*Notes on Anna Akhmatova*), 2 vols. (Paris: YMCA Press, 1976–80), 2:292.

2. Donchin, *Influence*, p. 156.

3. See Bryusov's "Kon' bled" ("The Pale Horse") and Blok's "Poslednii den'" ("The Last Day").

4. Alexander Blok, *Sobranie sochinenii* (*Collected Works*), (Moscow and Leningrad, 1960), 2:204.

5. "Neznakomka" ("The Stranger"), in ibid., p. 186.

6. Blok's "Beautiful Lady" is generally acknowledged to be indebted to the writings of the philosopher Vladimir Solovyov on the Divine Sophia. See O. Maslenikov, *The Frenzied Poets: Andrey Biely and the Russian Symbolists* (Berkeley and Los Angeles: University of California Press, 1952). According to Donchin, *Influence*, p. 162,

Blok's Lady is taken from Bryusov's poem "Prokhozhei" ("To a Woman Passer-by").

> 7.
> Akhmatova's Petersburg landscape was her poetic discovery. The "urbanism" of her predecessors, the Symbolists, took other paths. Thus, Bryusov continued the tradition of Verhaeren using the devices of metaphoric estrangement; he romantically poeticized the monstrous and fabled contemporary city. In Blok, for example, in the ballad "The Stranger," the city is presented in the distortion of a romantic grotesque. Akhmatova's Petersburg is shown realistically, but at the same time monumentally, in the classical Pushkinian manner, in which personal reminiscences intertwine with national history. [V. M. Zhirmunsky, *Tvorchestvo Anny Akhmatovoi* (*The Work of Anna Akhmatova*) (Leningrad, 1973), pp. 97–98]

8. See Antsiferov, *Dusha Peterburga*, p. 209: "In the quiet before the storm, there arose a poet who looked affectionately into the face of the doomed city and described it with tenderness, as a participant in its life."

Sam Driver, in *Anna Akhmatova* (New York: Twayne, 1972), p. 77, wrote: "Akhmatova is extremely receptive to the Petersburg mystique, to the great literary tradition and rich and colorful cultural history of the city. Unlike the Symbolists, however, she does not proceed from mystique to mystery. Her direction is opposite, toward the simplicity and clarity of concrete images. While the grandeur and magnificence—and the malevolence—are deeply sensed, Akhmatova's predominant attitude is a familiar one, even proprietary." See his general treatment of Akhmatova's Petersburg, pp. 73–82.

9. Driver, *Anna Akhmatova*, p. 75.

10. Zhirmunsky, *Tvorchestvo*, p. 73.

11. Leonid Grossman wrote of Akhmatova's cities: "These 'stone beauties,' to use Turgenev's words, not only serve as background for those love tales which are locked into the economical lines of Akhmatova's fragments; they are also material, in itself valuable, for her remarkable word-graphics" ("Anna Akhmatova," *Svitok* 4 [1926], p. 305; quoted in Driver, *Anna Akhmatova*, pp. 81–82).

12. David R. Weimar, *The City as Metaphor* (New York: Random House, 1966): "The cities in the works of fiction derive their significance *primarily* from within the individual works themselves"

(p. 3). "The categories we *most* require in order to deal with these cities are, therefore, not historical, sociological or epistemological, but metaphoric. . . . There are as many cities as there are imaginations" (p. 6).

13. Korney Chukovsky, "Anna Akhmatova" in *Sobranie sochinenii* (Collected Works), (Moscow, 1967), pp. 730–31.

14. Haight, *Akhmatova*, p. 44.

15. "The only way of expressing emotion in the form of art is by finding an 'objective correlative'; in other words, a set of objects, a situation, a chain of events which shall be the formula of that particular emotion; such that when the external facts are given, the emotion is immediately evoked" (T. S. Eliot, "Hamlet," in *Selected Essays*, 3d ed. [London: Faber and Faber, 1951], p. 145).

16. The concept of the shade—"ten'"—forms not only a sign of the return of the dead in the memory of the present . . . but is more regularly associated in Akhmatova's work with any transference in subjective consciousness of people and their relationships from one time level into another" (Kees Verheul, *The Theme of Time in the Poetry of Anna Akhmatova* [The Hague and Paris: Mouton, 1971], p. 7).

17. V. V. Vinogradov gives this line as an example of Akhmatova's linking of epithets from distant semantic categories; see *O poezii Anny Akhmatovoi* (*On the Poetry of Anna Akhmatova*), (Leningrad, 1925), p. 48.

18. The same paradigm, but in a lighter, nontragic register, lies at the basis of "Teper' proshchai, stolitsa" ("Now, farewell, capital," I/179–80, 1917). Here the heroine reluctantly contemplates leaving Petersburg, where "it is sweet to kiss him," for "the Karelian land." (Karelia is the region north of Leningrad, which forms a land bridge between Russia proper and the Finnish lake plateau.) The city is again the place of love; the speaker is leaving it with some regret. There is no indication of a love affair's tragic end; rather, we sense natural processes pulling her away; spring has come and she should be off to the country.

19. See Vinogradov, *O poezii*, pp. 52–54, for his analysis of this poem, tracing the vacillation of the epithet "last"—"poslednii" between two meanings: the most recent in an ongoing series (i.e., nontragic) and the final, or last (tragic). This duality resolves itself in the poem's final line, according to Vinogradov, in the direction of tragedy.

20. Ibid., p. 53.

21. Verheul, *Theme of Time*, pp. 11–12.

22. Ibid., p. 11.

23. The "again" of Akhmatova's line "Again St. Isaac's is in vestments" may be a reminiscence of Tyutchev's "I saw, standing above the Neva":

Глядел я, стоя над Невой,

Как Исаака-великана

Во мгле морозного тумана

Светился купол золотой.

I saw, standing above the Neva,
How the golden cupola of St. Isaac's-the-Giant
Shown brightly
In the darkness of the frosty mist.

24. An interesting contrast to this vision of Petersburg as the city of "dark blessing" is found in a poem of the following year, "Budem vmeste, milyi, vmeste" ("We will be together, love, together," I/147, 1915), in which the notions of "love's blessing" and "the dark city" (not specifically designated as Petersburg) are separated and made inimical to one another. The place of betrothal is described as a glistening church whose violent radiance could have been brought only by angels in white wings. This blessed church located in an unremembered place in an unspecified past is contrasted with the accursed present, defined as merged time/place:

А теперь пора такая,

Страшный год и страшный город.

And now is such a time,
Terrible year and terrible city.

In "Vsë otniato: i sila i liubov'" ("All has been taken: both strength and love," I/159, 1916), we find the line

В немилый город брошенное тело

Не радо солнцу.

Thrown into an unloved city, the body
Does not rejoice in the sun.

The poem was written in Sevastopol, which may be the "unloved city" referred to. There is nothing in the poem to suggest Petersburg. It is interesting, however, as another instance of the paradigm of the city as the place of nonlove.

25. See Alexis Rannit, "Anna Akhmatova Considered in a Context of Art Nouveau," *Sochineniia*, ed. Struve and Filippov, 2:5–38, for a discussion of the "Japanese" element in Akhmatova's early poetry. He quotes the poem under discussion as "being the most 'Japanese' in its brevity and symbolic force among Akhmatova's early poems" and one that "shows convincingly that Akhmatova can write in the Japanese tradition, in which imagery of nature is the crucial vehicle of meaning."

26. An interesting comparison with this poem is the later "Da, ia liubila ikh, te sborishcha nochnye" ("Yes, I loved them, those night gatherings," I/167, 1917), in which the speaker's attitude toward this same nightlife is one of fond reminiscence.

27. For a quintessential formulation of Petersburg in apocalyptic images, as the demonic incarnation of alien, Western elements, see Evgeny Ivanov's essay, "Vsadnik: nechto o gorode Peterburge" ("The Horseman: Something about the City of Petersburg"), published in the Petersburg almanac *Belye nochi* (*White Nights*), (Petersburg, 1907), 1:73–91. Blok fixed this negative historical image of the city in two poems of 1904 (originally published as "A Petersburg Poema"): "Pëtr" ("Peter") containing ominous, negative images of the emperor's power; and "Poedinok" ("The Duel") in which the symbolic historical enmity of Petersburg and Moscow is envisioned as a battle between Peter the Anti-Christ and the patron of Muscovite Rus, St. George. The apocalyptic vision of the city is a major thread running through Andrey Bely's masterpiece *Peterburg*. Also cf. Annensky's and Gippius's negative poems "Peterburg."

28. See "Chem khuzhe etot vek predshestvuiushchikh?" ("In what way is this age worse than others?" I/188, 1919), in which she uses the folklore image of "the white one" ("belaia") for death. The expression "white death" occurs in "Golos pamiati" ("The Voice of Memory," I/104, 1913).

29. Akhmatova's poem dramatizes the question of Tyutchev's "On the Neva," about the "mysterious barque" which carries off "two ghosts":

И опять звезда ныряет
В легкой зыби невских волн,

И опять любовь вверяет
Ей таинственный свой челн.

И меж зыбью и звездою
Он скользит, как бы во сне,
И два призрака с собою
Вдаль уносит по волне.

Дети ль это праздной лени
Тратят здесь досуг ночной?
Иль блаженные две тени
Покидают мир земной?

Ты, разлитая, как море,
Пышно-струйная волна,
Приюти в твоем просторе
Тайну скромного челна!

And again a star dives
In the ripple of the Neva waves,
And again love entrusts to it
Its mysterious barque.

And between the ripple and the star
It glides, as if in a dream,
And carries off with it
Along the wave two ghosts.

Are these children of vain indolence
Squandering here their nocturnal leisure?
Or two blessed shades
Abandoning the earthly sphere?

You, overflowing like the sea,
Luxuriantly flowing wave,
Preserve in your spaciousness
The secret of the modest barque!

30. Another unusual poem, in which the poet finds herself "in the midst of love's happiness." "Prosypat'sia na rassvete" ("To awaken at dawn," I/180, 1917) also takes place in a watery setting whose "green wave" suggests the Neva (cf. Mandelstam's "Mne

kholodno. Prozrachnaia vesna . . ." ["I am cold. Transparent spring
. . .], where the Neva is evoked in the image of "the heavy emerald
of the sea water"). The heroine is aboard a ship, where the premoni-
tion of a meeting fills her with youth and happiness:

> Но предчувствуя свиданье
>
> С тем, кто стал моей звездою,
>
> От соленых брызг и ветра
>
> С каждым часом молодеть.

> *But divining a meeting*
>
> *With him, who has become my star,*
>
> *From the salty spray and wind*
>
> *To grow younger with each hour.*

This is the antithesis of the closing lines of "Vizhu vytsvetshii flag
nad tamozhnei" ("I see the faded flag above the customs house,"
I/107, 1913):

> И не знать, что от счастья и славы
>
> Безнадежно дряхлеют сердца.

> *And not to know that from happiness and fame*
>
> *Hearts grow irreparably weak.*

Happiness and fame make the heart wither; the mild adversity of
salty spray and wind are invigorating—in the presence of love. In-
terestingly, "To awaken at dawn" is not told in the past tense: "I
awakened at dawn." The use of the infinitive expresses instead
strong desire, as it does in the quoted lines from "I see the faded
flag." The poem thus expresses a wish for this moment of fulfillment
in the midst of the waters rather than relating its occurrence. The
guilt and anxiety accompanying the reality ("Flight") are wholly ab-
sent in the wish.

31. See Antsiferov, *Dusha Peterburga*, p. 211: "Thus the Ger-
man romantics hoped for a meeting in Rome with their betrothed,
eternally predestined. In the eternal city there is no place for acci-
dent, everything acquires a sacred meaning, everywhere the pres-
ence of something great is sensed. Except that Akhmatova's vision is
free of romantic puffs of smoke."

The Historical City in Transition

In March 1914 my second book, Rosary, *was published. It had a life of roughly six weeks. In the beginning of May, the Petersburg season began to die, little by little, everyone scattered. This time separation from Petersburg turned out to be forever. We returned not to Petersburg, but to Petrograd; from the nineteenth century we were transported directly to the twentieth. Everything was different, beginning with the appearance of the city. It seemed that the little book of love lyrics by a beginning author was to drown in world events. Time decreed otherwise.*

    —Anna Akhmatova, "Korotko o sebe"
      ("Briefly About Myself")

It isn't the city of Rome which lives amidst the ages
But man's place in the universe.
    —Osip Mandelstam

II

As in a mirror, I glanced anxiously
At the gray canvas, and with each passing week,
More bitter and strange was the similarity
Between myself and my new image.

*A*khmatova's city materialized as an independent, historical theme, not as Saint Petersburg (1703–1914), but as the Petrograd (1914–1924) of World War I, the Bolshevik Revolution, and the Civil War. Yet not once in her poetry of those years does the name Petrograd appear. There are no Bolsheviks on the streets of Akhmatova's revolutionary city, no troops storming the Winter Palace. No inflammatory slogans deface the silent dignity of her city's buildings. Topical details, specific political or ideological allusions (such as one finds, for instance, in the revolutionary Petrograd of Blok's *The Twelve*), are almost wholly absent in her poetry of Petersburg's cataclysmic years. Indeed, the events shaping Akhmatova's poetic vision of the historical city during the Petrograd decade are present in the poems themselves only in the generalized sense of an embattled world in the throes of radical transformation.

Akhmatova's approach is at once personal and universal. As in her love lyrics, she continues to speak as one for whom the city is a place of fateful encounters. But the meetings of lovers are here overshadowed by the coming together of another "we"—whom she called, in one poem, "fellow citizens" ("sograzhdane"). In Akhmatova's usage, the term implies a group with which she shares both an irrecoverable loss and an unshakable loyalty. For the abrupt transformation of the face of the city, signifying the loss of the old life, sparked in her poetry an affirmation of the ideal City, a pure essence of ongoing community, which belongs to Petersburg but is greater than any specific incarnation of it.

The strong partisan resonance of these poems, then, has nothing to do with conventional political allegiances; like the dwellers of the earliest cities, Akhmatova dedicates herself to serving the city's "gods," "that divine object [which] sanctified every sacrifice, counteracted every abnegation."[1] As a refugee from the nineteenth to the "True Twentieth Century" city, however, she was obliged to formulate her own definition of that divinity.

Prelude: Autobiographical Myths

The discovery of Petersburg as an ultimate spiritual value came to Akhmatova, not through abstract philosophical speculation, but through that need to articulate the dimensions of her personal life, which lay at the very basis of her poetic impulse. The intimate link between the poet and her city, forged in the Petersburg love lyrics, took on greater scope during the years of historical upheaval, as she assigned the city the central role in her autobiographical myths. In two key poems of this period, Petersburg became the definition of an abruptly interrupted inner journey.

The earlier, briefer poem "Byl blazhennoi moei kolybel'iu" ("The dark city on the terrible river," I/126, 1914) is a love poem to Petersburg, the "city loved with a bitter love." The notion of a "dark blessing," present in the love poems, here permeates the speaker's sense of the significant stages of her life:

Был блаженной моей колыбелью
Темный город у грозной реки

The dark city on the terrible river
Was my blessed cradle

While the "darkness" of the city is conveyed through traditional, almost stylized epithets ("dark," "stern," "tranquil," "misty"), the city's "blessedness" is evoked through a series of unusual images of furniture: the city is "blessed cradle," marriage bed, and religious altar:

И торжественной брачной постелью,
Над которой держали венки
Молодые твои серафимы, —
Город, горькой любовью любимый.

Солеёю молений моих
Был ты, строгий, спокойный, туманный.

And the solemn bridal bed
Over which your young seraphims
Held wreaths,—
City, loved with a bitter love.

You were the prie-dieu
Of my prayers, stern, calm, misty.

This association of religious imagery with Petersburg, noted in the love poems as well, is distinctly Akhmatova's. Here it is connected with the sanctity accompanying the procession of life's pivotal stages. But the sequence of wholeness—cradle, marriage bed, altar—unexpectedly breaks off. Two unions are described:

Там впервые предстал мне жених,
Указавший мой путь осиянный,
И печальная Муза моя
Как слепую водила меня.

There my bridegroom first appeared to me,
He who showed me my illuminated path,
And my sad Muse led me
As if I were a blind woman.

One of Akhmatova's eloquent moments of reticence separates these two unions. In the final image, wholeness has given way to deformity: the blessed child and wife is now a blind woman; instead of an illuminated path, there is darkness. The speaker's blindness is related to the mistiness of the city. For Petersburg has been described as "stern, calm, misty," a series of epithets whose first two members (emotional) convey a sense of the city's *inner certainty*, while the third (physical) suggests *uncertainty*, lack of clarity for those living within the city. The images of blindness and the Muse, while confirming and deepening the city's "darkness," also represent the "blessing" of poetry, which makes a path through that darkness, revealing that which lies beyond the visible.

In considering this poem, it is essential to note that Petersburg was not, in fact, Akhmatova's birthplace, the city of her childhood, or the place where she met her first bridegroom (if we allot that role to Gumilyov). While Tsarskoe Selo, her childhood home, plays another, more specialized role in her poetry,[2] Akhmatova designates Petersburg as her spiritual birthplace.[3]

If "The dark city on the terrible river" is shaped by an impulse toward symbolic generalization, an opposing impulse toward expansive, narrative reminiscence dominates "Epicheskie motivy" ("Epic Motifs," I/191–194; part 1, 1913; part 2, 1915; part 3, 1914–1916).[4] In the first of these blank verse fragments, the poet describes the intense joy of her "pagan childhood" and her first meetings with the Stranger-Muse, who alternately offers and withdraws her precious gifts. The setting is a warm seaside place, possibly the Crimea, where Akhmatova spent her childhood summers.

In part 2 she comes to Petersburg, having abandoned this "sacred homeland" and "the Muse of Lamentation." Thus a very different myth of personal origins from the one we have seen in "The dark city on the terrible river" is developed here. In the former poem, Petersburg is the image of the integral, solemn procession of her life, culminating in her dependence upon the "sad Muse." Here we have, not a unified procession, but disparate stages. The sad Muse appears in the earliest period of her life, by the seashore. In a reversal of its usual "sternness," Petersburg is the domain of a more lighthearted Muse:

> Я, тихая, веселая, жила
> На низком острове, который, словно плот,
> Остановился в пышной Невской дельте.

О зимние таинственные дни,

И милый труд, и легкая усталость,

И розы в умывальном кувшине!

I, quiet, gay, lived
On a low island, which, like a raft,
Had stopped in the splendid Neva delta.
Oh, mysterious winter days,
And beloved labor, and faint tiredness,
And roses in the wash basin!

The heroine's intimacy with the river, afloat (yet at rest) on her island-raft in the middle of the Neva, is a position Akhmatova associates with fulfillment (cf. "Flight" and "To Awaken at Dawn"). The joyousness of these lines is undiluted, but if it is love's happiness which is implied, then the only clues to this are the roses in the washbasin and an isolated reference to a "we" ("and opposite our door"). This is a poem not of erotic love (for Akhmatova almost always an experience mixed with pain) but of a lighter, more innocent time of the soul. Images of freshness (the untouched snow——pale, clean sheets of snow) and tenderness (schooners, like doves, tenderly, tenderly pressed to one another) which accompany the heroine's morning walks from her house to the house of the artist[5]—invite such an interpretation, as does the poem's final image of their Muses:[6]

Но чувствую, что Музы наши дружны

Беспечной и пленительною дружбой,

Как девушки, не знавшие любви.

But I feel that our Muses are friendly,
With a carefree and enchanting friendship,
Like young girls who have not known love.

But if Petersburg is evoked as an age of innocence, it is a *lost* age, and darker overtones building toward that loss appear soon after the poem's idyllic beginning. (Although the snow's whiteness is suggested visually, the only color specifically mentioned is gray: the gray of the unreachable dockside and of the canvas on which the heroine discovers her double.) On that same walk to the artist's house, images of *elusiveness* (her inability to find yesterday's footsteps in the snow) and *confinement* (the snowbound schooner's longing for the gray dockside) appear, which are echoed in the image of the artist himself in his cagelike room,

> Где он, как чиж, свистал перед мольбертом
> И жаловался весело и грустно
> О радости небывшей говорил.

> *Where he, like a siskin, whistled in front of the easel*
> *And complained gaily and sadly*
> *Spoke of nonexistent happiness.*

If these images of evasion, absence, and nontouching have a mild, elegiac quality, the poem's single sharply disturbing image involves, instead, a recurrent moment of confrontation:

> Как в зеркало, глядела я тревожно
> На серый холст, и с каждою неделей
> Все горше и страннее было сходство
> Мое с моим изображеньем новым.

> *As in a mirror, I glanced anxiously*
> *At the gray canvas, and with each passing week,*
> *More bitter and strange was the similarity*
> *Between myself and my new image.*

If the shaping of life by art is the theme of these lines, then the self the heroine sees in the "mirror" of the canvas causes her to *recognize* the existence of "the other" within herself, which in turn becomes more clearly manifest in her life. The anxiety, strangeness, and bitterness associated with this recognition suggest the discovery of a dark double, but Akhmatova does not develop this traditional (Gogolian, Dostoevskian) Petersburg theme. The suggestion of a dawning self-knowledge which will put an end to the idyll is immediately followed by the line

Теперь не знаю, где художник милый,

Now I don't know where the dear artist is,

which separates the ominous portrait from its "dear" creator, restores the previous elegiac tone, and confirms the loss of this period of her life. Like the perilous ascent of heroine and artist to the roof "to see the snow, Neva and clouds," which the heroine now "recollects in tranquillity," the frightening portrait is framed within the tranquil tone of the poem as a whole.

The Petersburg of this poem is thus a second home to which the heroine comes after leaving her sacred homeland, where the Muse of Lamentation pines; it is a winter place of freshness, tenderness—a lost age of innocence, as well as the place of discovery, through art, of a darker, mirror self.

The third part of "Epic Motifs" does not represent a third stage in the heroine's life. Like the interrupted procession of "The dark city on the terrible river," the structure of "Epic Motifs" embodies the sense of sudden disruption of life's natural course. For part 3 represents the recollection of a single deeply satisfying moment in the city. In the poem's concluding lines (added in 1940), that moment is perceived as the far boundary of happiness, to be treasured in memory in the difficult years ahead.[7]

From the present winter moment, specifically located in Petersburg through the mention of a church, the speaker remembers a strange stroll through the city. An indefinable, mysterious quality of light and air, which

Так каждый звук лелеял и хранил,
Что мнилось мне: молчанья не бывает.

So cherished and preserved each sound,
That it seemed to me: silence does not exist.

and the sight of children on a bridge feeding ducks—give the
sense of "the fullness of spiritual powers and the charm of
the dear life." Petersburg's role as the locus of a homey, "do-
mestic" happiness is notable here; for, as we shall see, in
Akhmatova's postwar geography of human destiny, "the sim-
ple life" is specifically designated "non-Petersburg."

Transformation of the Old City

The underlying sense of a lost Petersburg era, which per-
vades parts 2 and 3 of "Epic Motifs," is made explicit in "Tot
golos, s tishinoi velikoi sporia" ("That voice, arguing with the
great silence," I/136, 1914) and is specifically identified with
the war. The "we" for whom Akhmatova speaks seems to
lie somewhere between a larger community—all those who
lived through that last winter—and a more intimate "we," for
whom that time period possessed the special intensity and
associations with which Akhmatova endows it:

Белее сводов Смольного собора,
Таинственней, чем пышный Летний сад,
Она была.

Whiter than the domes of the Smolny Cathedral,
More mysterious than the splendid Summer Garden
It was.

These images do more than localize the last winter in Peters-
burg and suggest private memories. They equate the sub-
jective quality of that time with the qualities of Petersburg

places, merging them indissolubly in time/place images of great intensity: to be whiter than the Smolny domes and more mysterious than the Summer Garden is to possess whiteness and mysteriousness in very high degree. The final lines

Не знали мы, что скоро
В тоске предельной поглядим назад.

We did not know that soon
In extreme anguish, we would look back.

which allude "to a future which was then not realized, and from which the past acquires a completely different meaning in retrospect,"[8] is general enough to imply both the agony of war and the private torment of the more intimate "we."

In a related poem of the following year, "Tot avgust, kak zheltoe plamia" ("That August, like a yellow flame," I/194, 1915), another time, in this instance, a time of war, is compared first to a "yellow flame, penetrating the smoke," and then to a "fiery seraphim":

Тот август, как желтое пламя,
Пробившееся сквозь дым,
Тот август поднялся над нами,
Как огненный серафим.

That August, like a yellow flame,
Penetrating through the smoke,
That August rose above us,
Like a fiery seraphim.

Here, too, private and public significances merge. The "fiery seraphim" belong to the series of "angel" images in poems of this period through which Akhmatova conveys the sense of destiny—either positive or negative—hovering above her love affairs: Petersburg's "young seraphims" which blessed

her marriage bed (I/126); "God's Angel," who watched over
her dark-hued Petersburg love (I/128); and the sharp-winged
"black angels" auguring the approach of a Last Judgment
(I/126). In this poem, however, the seraphim must also be
seen as symbolic of the apocalyptic time of war. More exten-
sively than in "That voice arguing with the great silence,"
Akhmatova weaves private and public threads into a single
tapestry. The man and woman around whom the narrative re-
volves are generalized as "warrior and maid" and the trans-
formation of their lives by the general cataclysm is paralleled
by the transformation of their city. For the first time in Akh-
matova's poetry, Petersburg is described as "the city of sad-
ness and anger":

И в город печали и гнева
Из тихой Карельской земли
Мы двое — воин и дева —
Студеным утром вошли.

And to the city of sadness and anger,
From the quiet Karelian earth,
We two—warrior and maid—
Came on a frozen morning.[9]

Although "sadness" comes close to the "gloominess" which
is traditionally linked with the city and which Akhmatova fre-
quently adopts in the evocation of her "dark" city, the term
"anger" is truly out of character for Akhmatova's restrained,
stern, and calm city. Petersburg's lofty tranquillity is now re-
placed by negative, violent human emotions. The speaker
asks:

Что сталось с нашей столицей,
Кто солнце на землю низвел?
Казался летящей птицей
На штандарте черный орел.

What happened to our capital,
Who lowered the sun to earth?
The black eagle on the standard
Seemed like a bird in flight.

Petersburg is still "our capital" but is caught in a distortion which appears as a destruction of form.[10] In an apocalyptic image, sun and earth, meant to be separate, converge. The black eagle, which seems to come to life, is not an image of the imperial symbol taking on new vitality. In losing its symbolic quality, the eagle on the standard represents a regressive process: form violating its fixed nature, civilization returning to wilderness.[11] Akhmatova has cherished Petersburg as the city of eternal forms and civilized rituals. Now this structure is threatened.

In the lines:

На дикий лагерь похожим
Стал город пышных смотров,

The city of splendid military reviews
Has become like a wild camp,

she signals that transformation of the city "into the opposite of itself" about which she would later write in her reminiscences of Mandelstam and of Petersburg in the early 1920s:

All of the old Petersburg signboards were still in their places, but there was nothing behind them except dust, gloom and yawning emptiness. Typhus, hunger, execution, darkness in the apartments, damp firewood, people swollen to unrecognizability. In the Gostiny Dvor one could collect a huge bouquet of field flowers. The famous Petersburg wooden pavements were rotting. The smell of chocolate still emanated from the basement windows of Kraft's. All of the cemeteries had been vandalized. The city had not simply changed; it had decidedly turned into its opposite.[12]

In her 1915 vision of the city transformed by war, where the sound of "thundering" gray cannons drowns out the "booming" Troytsky Bridge,[13] only nature remains true to itself:

А липы еще зеленели
В таинственном Летнем саду.

But the lindens were still green
In the mysterious Summer Garden.

The term "nature" must be qualified, however, for this is the special "shaped" nature of the Summer Garden, which figured in Akhmatova's 1913 evocation of the city's eternal rituals ("Verses about Petersburg"). The term "mysterious" applied to the Summer Garden here, and in "That voice, arguing with the great silence" is an epithet Akhmatova has also applied to Petersburg days as well as to the "mysterious song gift" of poetry. For Akhmatova, mystery is a characteristic of form; the Summer Garden is the single refuge of that form which seems to have vanished from the city. The warrior departs, leaving the maid to preserve their sadness and happiness:

Как будто ключи оставил
Хозяйке усадьбы своей,
А ветер восточный славил
Ковыли приволжских степей.

As if he were leaving the keys
To the mistress of his country estate,
And the eastern wind sang the praises
Of the feathergrass of the Volga steppe.

According to Verheul, this concluding folklore formula "does not stand in contrast to the military activity of the town, but forms a concluding and unifying image of Russian patriotism."[14] Yet "Russia" here is represented by desolate nature, devoid of men. There is no poet praising his city; Peter's city has vanished, and what remains is a wind, blowing from the direction of Old Russia's traditional Asian invaders; here the wilderness whispers to itself.

A poem written six years later develops this theme of the city's transformation from a point in time after the devastation, whose beginning is evoked in the 1915 poem, is already complete. "Vsë raskhishcheno, predano, prodano" ("All is plundered, betrayed, sold out," I/201, 1921) begs comparison with the previously discussed "A fantastic autumn" (1922). Written in the years of devastation after the Civil War, both poems evoke a barely recognizable Petersburg whose stones have been overrun by a luxuriant, revitalized nature.[15] Like the "fantastic autumn" of the 1922 poem, in "All is plundered" a "fantastic forest near the city" expresses the heightening of nature which presages the approach of the miraculous. In contrast to the concluding image of a human figure, a "you" ("ty") who approaches the speaker's porch, here, the miraculous possesses an abstract, public quality:

> И так близко подходит чудесное
> К развалившимся грязным домам...
> Никому, никому неизвестное,
> Но от века желанное нам.

> *And the miraculous approaches so closely*
> *The dilapidated dirty houses . . .*
> *Known to no one, to no one,*
> *But forever desired by us.*

The sense of the miraculous associated with Akhmatova's Petersburg ("Peter's miraculous city," "the blessed moment of miracles" in the Summer Garden), here acquires the meaning of salvation arising from the very depth of despair. In applying to Petersburg this concept, whose roots may be traced to Russian Orthodox theories of kenoticism,[16] Akhmatova suggests a reversal of the tradition of the city as the cursed, barren place, the city of the anti-Christ; her city has a phoenixlike capacity for rebirth from its own ashes.

This linking of Petersburg with an inherent capacity for salvation occurs as well in "Vysokomer'em dukh tvoi pomrachën" ("Your spirit is clouded by arrogance," I/165, 1917), in which the city is an integral part of the speaker's defense of Russia against an unidentified foreign addressee:

Ты говоришь, что вера наша — сон,
И марево — столица эта.

You say that our faith is a dream,
And this capital a mirage.

The accusation that "this capital is a mirage," though not directly addressed, is by implication, like all the rest the "outsider" says, refuted. Petersburg is identified with Russia, and Russia in this poem is a beggarly sinnerwoman who has been given the possibility of fully atoning for her sins; she is whole in spirit, as opposed to the wealthy, godless country of the addressee.

Petersburg itself is the "sinner" in a poem of the preceding year, "Kak liubliu, kak liubila gliadet' ia" ("How I love, how I loved to look," I/154, 1916). Unlike the programmatic "defense" of the previous poem, from which the religious imagery arises, here the imagistic formulation of the city's spirituality is born from its sensual impact upon the speaker. The poem begins with a puzzling declaration of love past and present—puzzling, because it is unclear whether her past love refers to a specific time or to the fact that she has always loved. The absence of such words as "forever" and "always" makes the former possibility more likely, but Akhmatova does not pursue the private allusion:

> Как люблю, как любила глядеть я
> На закованные берега,
> На балконы, куда столетья
> Не ступала ничья нога.

> *How I love, how I loved to look*
> *At the enchained shores,*
> *At the balconies where for centuries*
> *No one's foot has stepped.*

For Akhmatova, Petersburg is almost always the Neva, the palace, monuments, the majestic public side of the city. But it becomes particularized, sometimes through specific private detail—such as the balconies on which no one has set foot for centuries—and often, as in the second half of the poem, through the intoxicating confluence of a particular time of day, a special weather, a haunting quality of light and air. Here, this finely perceived city gives rise to two definitions of itself: the first, in terms of those whose capital it is:

> И воистину ты — столица
> Для безумных и светлых нас;

> *And in truth you are the capital*
> *For us mad and radiant ones;*

This "we" is thus a spiritual elite, perhaps poets, possessors of that "radiant madness" of the holy fool ("iurodivyi") whose antics conceal a higher wisdom. The connection between this radiant madness and the city images leading up to it seems to lie in an irrational yet compelling aspect of the city's forms and rituals: the enchained banks, the empty balconies, images of the external city which both confirm and conform to the inner state of its spiritual inhabitants.

The second definition of the city is in terms of its own subjective experience:

Но, когда над Невою длится
Тот особенный, чистый час
И проносится ветер майский
Мимо всех надворных колонн,
Ты — как грешник, видящий райский
Перед смертью сладчайший сон...

But when above the Neva
That special pure hour stretches out
And the May wind blows through,
Past all the outer columns,
You are like a sinner, seeing an intensely sweet,
Deathbed dream of paradise . . .

Although the conjunction "but" ("no") sets up a contrast between the two definitions of the city, they are actually variations on the same theme, which the poet reaches, however, through different channels: the first, through the observation of architecture, the second, through a less tangible sense of atmosphere. The sinner's dream is pierced by the "radiance" of paradise. Its "madness" is sweet delusion; for a sinner's deathbed dream of paradise speaks, not of salvation, but of the yearning for salvation. It is important that Akhmatova does not compare the city itself to a dream of paradise but instead personifies it in this way. A sense of pathos envelops the city-sufferer, itself wrapped in a blissful, delusive dream.

Petersburg's Proud, Tragic Fate and "the Simple Life"

Thus in the years of war and revolution, Akhmatova first saw Petersburg as a city transformed into the opposite of itself, civilization returned to wilderness. From the desolation of that wilderness, she foresaw the approach of the miraculous and evoked the suffering city in terms of transgression and salvation, always insisting upon its radiant spiritual vitality.

In these years, Akhmatova also formulated the counterbalance to this religious optimism: a sense of Petersburg as the symbol and incarnation of a proud, tragic destiny. In "Ved' gde-to est' prostaia zhizn' i svet" ("Surely somewhere there is a simple life and light," I/149, 1915) the contrast between two fates is embodied in the spatial dichotomy of the "splendid granite city of glory and misfortune" and the country setting of "the simple life."[17] They do not exist on equal planes, however, for the existence of the simple life is only a hypothesis:

> Ведь где-то есть простая жизнь и свет,
> Прозрачный, теплый и веселый...
> Там с девушкой через забор сосед
> Под вечер говорит, и слышат только пчелы
> Нежнейшую из всех бесед.

> *Surely somewhere there is a simple life and light/world,*
> *Transparent, warm and gay . . .*
> *There a neighbor talks with a young girl*
> *Over a fence at dusk and only the bees*
> *Hear this most tender of all conversations.*[18]

It is difficult to imagine Akhmatova tempted by this static love scene, lacking both tension and grandeur. Hers is the world, not of simplicity, but of paradox:

> А мы живем торжественно и трудно
> И чтим обряды наших горьких встреч,
> Когда, с налету, ветер безрассудный
> Чуть начатую обрывает речь, —

> *But we live solemnly and arduously*
> *And honor the rituals of our bitter meetings,*

When a gust of reckless wind
Cuts off a barely begun speech,—

In Petersburg, significance and pain ("solemnly and arduously") are inseparable. *Structure* (rituals, "obriady") is inseparable from *obstruction*: for in contrast to the uninterrupted conversation of girl and neighbor, between whom stands only the negligible barrier of a wooden fence, the speech of Petersburg's bitter meetings is interrupted as soon as it is begun by the "reckless wind" of sudden adversity.

In the poet's embracing of this Petersburg fate, in the final stanza, the elements which constitute the "simple life" are transposed into paradoxical complexities:

Но ни на что не променяем пышный
Гранитный город славы и беды,
Широких рек сияющие льды,
Бессолнечные, мрачные сады
И голос Музы еле слышный.

But not for anything would we exchange our splendid
Granite city of glory and misfortune,
The glistening ice of broad rivers,
The sunless, gloomy gardens
And the barely audible voice of the Muse.

Akhmatova's "pyshnyi, granitnyi gorod slavy i bedy" ("splendid granite city of glory and misfortune") echoes Pushkin's "Gorod pyshnyi, gorod bednyi" ("Splendid city, poor city").[19] In Pushkin's conceptualization, however, the splendor and poverty of the city are juxtaposed; in Akhmatova, they are merged. In contrast to the "simple life and light," these images merge opposing semantic fields: lavishness and austerity (splendid, granite); victory and defeat (glory, misfortune); massiveness and fragility (broad rivers, glistening ice); warmth and cold (glistening, ice); light and darkness, abundance and barrenness (gardens, gloomy, sunless). The final image, carrying forward the notion of "interrupted speech" of stanza 2, is a variation on these oppositions:

near silence	*speech*
And the barely audible	voice of the Muse.

The Muse is not present at all in stanza 1. She lives, not in the static idyll, but in the city landscape where life and death are inseparable and her barely audible voice is overheard only at great cost.[20]

Thus as the image of Petersburg becomes central to Akhmatova's poetic conceptualization of her generation's fate, its harsh outlines stand out even more sharply against the accompanying vision of a simple life, a static image of easy, "normal" happiness. The simple life, paler and less inspiring than its tragic foil, continues to haunt Akhmatova's sense of a woman's fate. In "Lotova zhena" ("Lot's Wife," I/222, 1922–1924), it is embodied in "the red towers of native Sodom," the city of domestic happiness, where the woman sang, spun, and bore children to a dear husband. Yet the complexity of Akhmatova's vision of such a city is revealed by her choice of Sodom, the city destroyed because of its own iniquities, to play this role. The warm, gay, transparent light of the simple life is neither wholly separate nor immune from the surrounding darkness. This archetype of a "blessed city" from which the woman is excluded by the tragic events of history, will become a major theme later in Akhmatova's career, particularly in her long poem of Kitezh, "Putëm vsia zemli" ("The Way of All the Earth," I/242–246, 1940) and in the "Third Northern Elegy" "Menia, kak reku" ("Like a river, I," I/311, 1944).[21]

Lot's wife loses the "blessed city" after living in it for many years; Akhmatova never lived in it at all; her course, as she writes in the "Third Northern Elegy," was diverted at the outset, and the diversion is attributed to the "stern epoch."

Recalling the early Petersburg love poems, however, it seems clear that Akhmatova's heroine would have made a poor candidate for the ordinary life no matter what epoch she had lived in. As we have seen, the paradigm: "a bright, simple, peaceful realm, to which the heroine seeks entry, and a cold, turbulent one to which she belongs"—appeared early in her career, in connection with the search for love. Her exclusion from "the blessed city" is ordained by the futility of her unrequited love:

> Ты меня совсем не любишь,
> Не полюбишь никогда...
> Для чего же, бросив друга
> И кудрявого ребенка,
> Бросив город мой любимый
> И родную сторону,
> Черной нищенкой скитаюсь
> По столице иноземной?

> *You don't love me at all*
> *And you never will . . .*
> *Why, having left my friend*
> *And curly-haired child,*
> *Having left my beloved city,*
> *And my homeland,*
> *Do I wander, a dark beggarwoman*
> *Through a foreign capital?*
> *[I/184, 1917]*

She never appears as the contented wife and mother. As Haight notes, her early sense of herself as a mother is a negative one.[22] As mistress and wife she fails, too, and this failure is often attributed to her "abnormal" spiritual nature as witch and poet. As an individual, she incarnates the impossibility of having a "simple life." This is the essentially romantic theme of the solitariness of the extraordinary individual. In

Akhmatova's "feminine" adaptation of this theme, the "society" which rejects her as a misfit, and which she must ultimately reject as a denial of herself, is the world of love between men and women, with its "ordinary" demands and expectations. In the transformation of this theme of the fate of the extraordinary woman into the theme of national, historical destiny, Petersburg played a central role. For Akhmatova's private city of "dark blessing," with its mixed associations of sternness and generosity, deprivation and miracle, was ideally structured for the incorporation of new meanings associated with the national fate.

Two Cities

In "Verses about Petersburg," the attempt to find consolation for the failure of a love affair in the eternal life of the city, envisioned as a reassuring cultural continuity, is undermined by the coexistent vision of the city as "negative immobility," entrapment within a bounded space. As Akhmatova's historical sense of Petersburg evolved, these two visions remained; instead of undermining one another, however, the eternal city now enters into a new, triumphant relationship with the entrapping one.

The poem "Sograzhdanam" ("To My Fellow Citizens," I/213, 1923)[23] incorporates these two Petersburgs in almost programmatic fashion; for the speaker and her fellow citizens stand simultaneously within both the eternal city of holy, organic forms and the hellish city of a fixed, historical moment.

In stanza 1, the "we" are enclosed in a "wild capital" reminiscent of the "wild camp" of "That August, like a yellow flame":

> И мы забыли навсегда,
> Заключены в столице дикой,
> Озера, степи, города
> И зори родины далекой.

And we have forgotten for all times,
Imprisoned in the wild capital,
Lakes, steppes, cities
And dawns of our far-off motherland.

Here the "wild capital" is contrasted to the "homeland" of both nature and cities; it is a place of exile, a prison. If the next two lines are a description of civil war, they also suggest both the circular geometry and the endless torture of hell:

В кругу кровавом день и ночь
Долит жестокая истома:

In a bloody circle day and night,
A cruel languor reigns:

But these place definitions are suddenly reversed in the stanza's conclusion:

Никто нам не хотел помочь
За то, что мы остались дома.

No one wanted to help us
Because we stayed at home.

Exile has been redefined as home. Those who have been designated as prisoners, inmates of hell, now become the loyal fellow citizens of the poem's title:

За то, что, город свой любя,
А не крылатую свободу,
Мы сохранили для себя
Его дворцы, огонь и воду.

Because, loving our city,
And not winged freedom,

We preserved for ourselves
Its palaces, fire and water.

Freedom itself is redefined as a choice inferior to fidelity, imprisonment in the city as the noble act of preserving tradition at the cost of personal sacrifice. In preserving "for themselves" "palaces, fire and water"—the harmony of architecture and nature,[24] which Akhmatova substitutes for the air, earth, fire, and water of the Greeks, as the basic elements of the cosmos—the "we" of the poem have preserved themselves, for the city will stand as an unwitting monument to them:

Иная близится пора,
Уж ветер смерти сердце студит,
Но нам священный храм Петра
Невольным памятником будет.

Another time draws near,
Already the wind of death freezes the heart,
But Peter's holy temple
Will be an unwitting monument to us.

Confinement and *fixedness*, which have a negative meaning in stanza 1 ("imprisoned") and the first half of stanza 2 ("in a bloody circle") take on a positive meaning in the second half of stanza 2 ("we stayed home"), which is carried forward in the mutual preservation of city and citizens in stanzas 3 and 4. Correspondingly, *expansiveness* and *movement*, positive in stanza 1 (lakes, steppes, cities, the far-off homeland and, by implication, the ability to reach these places) become negative in stanza 3 in the "winged freedom" which is identified with lack of responsibility in preserving tradition, and in stanza 4 (the approach of "another time," the blowing of the wind of death).

The poem's imagery thus not only insists upon the co-existence of two cities; it establishes the crucial relationship between them. For in order to preserve the holy city it is necessary to remain within the hellish city of the fixed historical moment. Thus in the spatial dualities of her poetry, Akhmatova's allegiances are clear: life in "the splendid granite city of glory and misfortune" is a fate superior to the "simple life"; residence within that harsh city of historical necessity is the price of preserving the eternal city.

The Squandered Inheritance

The triumphant assertion of "To My Fellow Citizens" represents, however, not the culmination, but only a stage in Akhmatova's long poetic relationship with Petersburg-Leningrad. In time of embattlement, it is easier to see what must be fought for and preserved; in quieter, less dramatic years, what is valued most highly may slip away, imperceptibly. Thus in 1929, Akhmatova could awaken and suddenly perceive "Tot gorod, mnoi liubimyi s detstva" ("That city which I have loved since childhood," I/231–232) as her "squandered inheritance." The enumeration of that inheritance recapitulates the elements of her early autobiographical myth "The dark city on the terrible river," whose notion of "dark blessing" is here transposed into that of "unearned blessing":

> Все, что само давалось в руки,
> Что было так легко отдать:
> Душевный жар, молений звуки
> И первой песни благодать —

> *Everything which came of itself into my hands,*
> *Which was so easy to give away:*
> *Spiritual ardour, the sounds of prayer*
> *And the grace of first song—*

This past has already vanished "in the depths of the mirror"—here a repository of the bright, receding world, a reversal of the mirror-painting image of "Epic Motifs," which contains the dark, emergent self.[25] When this lost city returns, in the poem's final two stanzas, it does so through the perceptions of the speaker, who looks upon her familiar surroundings

> Но с любопытством иностранки,
> Плененной каждой новизной,

> *But with the curiosity of a foreigner,*
> *Enchanted by each novelty,*

The image of the foreigner suggests a sudden freshness of perception, but it also implies that the speaker is, in fact, one who resides in the foreign city of the present, Soviet Leningrad. It is in this foreign city that the miraculous reunion of the speaker and her old friend/city takes place:[26]

> И дикой свежестью и силой
> Мне счастье веяло в лицо,
> Как будто друг от века милый
> Всходил со мною на крыльцо.

> *And with wild freshness and strength*
> *Happiness wafted in my face,*
> *As if a dear old friend*
> *Had walked with me onto my porch.*

The semantic and verbal correspondences between this poem and the 1921 poem "All is plundered," which also ends with a miraculous arrival, are striking: a *forever* dear friend ("drug *ot veka* milyi") and the *forever* desired miracle ("*ot veka* zhelannoe nam").

Once the place of death and resurrection, Petersburg is now its subject. The resurrection of the city of the past, where loss is bound up both with history's impersonal processes and with an implacable personal guilt, becomes the major Petersburg theme of Akhmatova's later years.

Notes

1. Lewis Mumford, *The City in History* (New York: Harcourt, Brace and World, 1961), p. 94.

2. In her early poetry, the image of Tsarskoe Selo, where Akhmatova spent most of her childhood, is associated with Pushkin and the theme of art's transformation of suffering ("V Tsarskom Sele" ("In Tsarskoe Selo," I/62, 1911), and "Tsarskosel'skaia statuia" ("Tsarskoe Selo Statue," I/160, 1916). In other poems, Akhmatova's "little toy town" appears as a dreamlike realm, unconnected with the rest of reality. Images of the royal realm under a spell occur in "Pervoe vozvrashchenie" ("First Return," I/54–55, 1910), and in "Prizrak" ("The Ghost," I/201, 1919), which envisages the "return" of the dead tsar. The theme of Tsarskoe Selo's enormous park occurs in "Golos pamiati" ("The Voice of Memory," I/104–105, 1913), the poem dedicated to Olga Sudeykina, which alludes to the suicide of the young poet Vsevolod Knyazev, an incident Akhmatova would later develop as the kernel of *Poema bez geroia* (*Poem without a Hero*). Here Akhmatova designates the park as the place where "anxiety intersected your path." In the later "Russkii Trianon" ("Russian Trianon," I/341–42, 1923), the stillness of the park signifies the isolation of the royal realm and its imperviousness to the impending catastrophe of World War I. Tsarskoe Selo figures, as well, in two poems of 1915: "Son" ("Dream"), I/139–40, in which the poet's lover searches for her in a dream, in Tsarskoe Selo, and "Milomu" ("To the Beloved"), I/138, in which Tsarskoe Selo is the frozen realm of life viewed from the mobile, warm realm of death. Thus Tsarskoe Selo appears as a more isolated, dreamlike realm in the early poetry, as compared with Petersburg, which is the stage of love and historical destiny. In the later poetry, Petersburg and Tsarskoe Selo thematics converge in the evocation of the lost prewar era.

3. "The image of St. Petersburg is used . . . to evoke the harsher aspects of the poet's fate" (Haight, *Akhmatova*, p. 50).

4. The last eight lines were first published in 1943. "Mrs. Lidija Chukovskaja told me that according to her diaries the fragment in question must have been written between the eighth and twelfth of June 1940" (Verheul, *Theme of Time*, p. 16).

5. "Evidently this poem forms a reflection on the famous portrait of Akhmatova by Natan Al'tman and on the brief relationship between the two artists during the time at which it was being

painted. . . . As appears from a note in Akhmatova's memoirs of Amadeo Modigliani, the portrait by Al'tman was painted during the years 1914–1915. Cf. Anna Akhmatova: *Works*, Vol. II, p. 163. The poem . . . was therefore written relatively shortly after the events that form the external basis of its narrative" (Verheul, *Theme of Time*, p. 52).

6. Verheul speaks of this image as an "unexpectedly tragical comparison," perceiving it as a continuation of "the motif of frustrated love" (*Theme of Time*, p. 54). But these are young girls who have *not yet* known love. The permanence of their "carefree and captivating friendship" appears as a fixed symbol of the period of spiritual history to which Akhmatova pays homage in this reminiscence.

7. See Verheul, *Theme of Time*, pp. 15–17, for an analysis of the temporal perspective in this poem.

8. Ibid., p. 56.

9. See "Teper' proshchai, stolitsa" ("Now, farewell, capital," I/179, 1917), in which Karelia is the innocent country place contrasted with Petersburg, the place of love. For Karelia, see chapter 1, n. 18.

10. In the earliest variant to Akhmatova's "Kogda v toske samoubiistva" ("When in the anguish of suicide"), published in the daily newspaper *Volia Rossii* in 1918, she expressed the city's transformation in terms of the whore-Babylon image:

Когда приневская столица,
Забыв величие свое,
Как опьяневшая блудница,
Не знала, кто берет ее,

When the capital on the Neva,
Having forgotten its greatness,
Like a drunken whore
Did not know who was taking her,
[I, 378]

11. There is a fascinating correspondence between Akhmatova's eagle image and Mandelstam's 1917 image in "Dvortsovaia ploshchad'" ("Palace Square"):

Словно в воздухе струится
Желчь двуглавого орла.

> *As if the bile of the two-headed eagle*
> *Were streaming in the air.*

Much in Akhmatova's poems resonates with Mandelstam's sense of the city: his youthful admiration for military demonstrations, his later sense of the city's transformation into something foreign to its own nature. See "Cassandra" (1917), dedicated to Akhmatova, where he speaks of "the city gone mad," and "V Peterburge my soidemsia snova" ("We will meet again in Petersburg") (1920), where "the capital arches like a wild cat."

12. With minor alterations, the English translation is by Kristin A. De Kuiper, *Russian Literature Triquarterly* 9 (spring 1974), p. 244.

13. Troytsky Bridge (now Kirovsky): in 1900 the wooden bridge was replaced by a metal one, the biggest one in the central part of the city.

14. "Public Themes in the Poetry of Akhmatova," in *Tale without a Hero and Twenty-Two Poems by Anna Akhmatova* (Paris: Mouton, 1973), p. 37.

15. Mandelstam's 1921 vision of the transformation of the city inevitably comes to mind: "The grass in Petersburg's streets is the first sprouts of a virginal forest, which will cover the site of modern cities. This bright, tender verdure, astonishing in its freshness, belongs to a new inspired nature. In truth, Petersburg is the most advanced city in the world" ("Slovo i kul'tura" ["The Word and Culture"], in *Sobranie sochinenii v trëkh tomakh* (*Collected Works in Three Volumes*), ed. G.P. Struve and B.A. Filippov (Washington, D.C.: Inter-Language Literary Associates, 1964–71), 2:264.

16. See George P. Fedotov, *The Russian Religious Mind* (New York: Harper, 1946), pp. 390–95.

17. Pushkin offers an early paradigm for the contrast of a "simple life" and a tragic Petersburg fate in *Mednyi vsadnik* (*The Bronze Horseman*). The vision of the "simple life" occurs in Evgeny's musings on his future happiness with Parasha.

18. The Russian word "svet" has the meanings "light" and "world," both of which fit Akhmatova's poetic context here.

19.

> Город пышный, город бедный,
> Дух неволи, стройный вид,

Свод небес зелено-бледный,

Скука, холод и гранит —

Все же мне вас жаль немножко,

Потому что здесь порой

Ходит маленькая ножка,

Вьется локон золотой.

Splendid city, poor city,

Spirit of bondage, comely aspect,

Green-pale vault of the heavens,

Boredom, cold and granite—

Still, I grieve a bit to leave you,

Because here at times

A little foot walks,

A golden lock curls.

20. An analogous conception is found in a poem by Akhmatova's close friend M. Lozinsky, "Peterburg" (1912), in Afanasev, Zakharov, and Tomashevsky, comps, *Petersburg, Petrograd, Leningrad in Russian Poetry*, p. 201; Lozinsky's poem shows a preference for Petersburg's "difficult" life as compared with a new existence in far-off, scorching lands.

21. Cf. "Bezhetsk" (I/214, 1921), which presents another image of the "blessed city" from which the speaker is excluded. Painful memories of her life there with Gumilyov, executed in that year, exclude her from the city "full of gay Christmas sounds."

22. Haight, *Akhmatova*, p. 9.

23. *Stikhotvoreniia i poemy* includes this poem under the title "Petrograd, 1919." This edition contains two variations: "rodiny velikoi" ("great motherland") instead of "far-off motherland" and "sviashchënnyi grad Petra" ("Petra's holy city," "grad" being the archaic form of the word *city*), instead of "Peter's holy temple."

24. Once more, Akhmatova's conception of the city resonates with Mandelstam's. In his poem "The Admiralty," (1913), in *Collected Works* 1:29, the harmony of architecture and natural elements is conveyed in the image of the Admiralty Building as "brother of water and sky."

25. See Verheul, *Theme of Time*, p. 38, for a discussion of the mirror image in Akhmatova.

26. The image of the *"forever* dear friend" leaves room for alternative interpretations. To Verheul, the reference seems to be to "her partner from the earlier books" (*Theme of Time*, p. 85), while Lydia Chukovskaya has no doubts that Akhmatova is alluding to her relationship with the Russian language; see *Zapiski*, 2:34.

The Terror
and the War

Who can refuse to live his own life?
  —From a 1940 conversation
  with Lydia Chukovskaya

To live in Petersburg is to sleep in a grave.
  —Osip Mandelstam

Smoke drifts from under the tsar's stables,
The Moyka sinks into darkness,
The light of the moon seems purposely muted,
And where we're going—I cannot know.

*F*rom the mid-1920s, when her fifteen-year period of reduced poetic productivity began,[1] until her death in 1966, Leningrad remained both Akhmatova's official residence and the locus of her spiritual drama. From the 1950s onward, she came to spend a great deal of her time living "secretly" with friends in Moscow, because, she once explained to Amanda Haight, "Moscow loves me, Leningrad does not love me."[2] Yet it was the old capital whose image dominated the great synthetic vision of human history which obsessed the last quarter century of her life, her "Petersburg Tale," *Poem without a Hero*. While she was creating this major oeuvre, other Petersburg-Leningrads continued to rise from the plains of Akhmatova's poetic history: the city of the Terror; the Great Martyr of the war years; phoenix; memorial; eternal home; timeless city of nonmeetings. The city of love, which dominated the early Petersburg lyrics, reshaped itself to the contours of a city of the "True Twentieth Century," where lovers meet by the shores of the river Lethe-Neva.

The Prison City

Lydia Chukovskaya describes the following conversation with Akhmatova in February of 1939:

> We walk along the Fontanka, past the park, past the Engineer's Palace.
> —"Aren't you sick of Petersburg," she asks, after a long silence.
> —"I? No."
> —"But I am—very. The distances, houses—images of petrified suffering. And I haven't been away for so long, too long."[3]

By the end of the 1930s, countless friends had vanished into the Gulag; Akhmatova's third "husband," Nikolay Punin, and her son, Lev, had been arrested.[4]

It seems inevitable that the image of a city in Akhma-

tova's poetry of these years should depend upon the related
notions of exile and imprisonment. For as the above inter-
change indicates, the city denied to the exiled prisoner be-
comes the prison of those left behind.

It was in "Dante," (I/236, 1936) that Akhmatova ex-
plored the essential duality of the lost native city:

Он из ада ей послал проклятье
И в раю не мог ее забыть, —
Но босой, в рубахе покаянной,
Со свечей зажженной не прошел
По своей Флоренции желанной,
Вероломной, низкой, долгожданной...

From hell he sent her his curses,
And in heaven could not forget her,—
But barefoot, in a penitent's shirt,
With lit candle he did not pass
Through his longed-for Florence,
Treacherous, base, long-awaited . . .

If, earlier, Akhmatova had paid homage to Lot's wife, who
"gave her life for a single look back," here she sings her song
to the man who "leaving, did not look back." For Dante's exile
is the work not of God but of men, and his refusal to return,
even after death, is an assertion of his proud spirit and un-
willingness to reenter his native city on other than honorable
terms.[5] There is a striking correspondence between this poem
and Mandelstam's poem of the following year "Slyshu, sly-
shu rannii lëd" ("I hear, I hear the early ice") in which Man-
delstam fuses the images of his remembered Petersburg and
Dante's Florence in the "archetype of the native and accursed,
desired and inaccessible city of the banished poet."[6] This
similarity need not be explained on the basis of the direct in-
fluence of Akhmatova's poem, which Mandelstam is unlikely
ever to have read. For in 1933 Mandelstam and Akhmatova
were reading Dante's *Divina commedia* together in Italian.

Haight reports "To her delight, another proof of their close spiritual ties, they discovered that they had begun to read Dante at the same time, each without being aware that the other had done so."[7] If further proof is required of Mandelstam's presence in Akhmatova's poem about Dante, it may be found in her poem of the same year "Voronezh" (I/235). Petersburg, "the native and accursed city," is the missing center of both poems. Dante's Florence is its historical double; Voronezh, the city of Mandelstam's exile, its "frozen" antithesis. Mandelstam's poem of the previous year "Pusti menia, otdai menia, Voronezh" ("Let me go, give me back, Voronezh") is a relentless pulling at the sounds of "Voronezh," which conjures the image of the city as a powerful, arbitrary, deadly thing: "Voronezh—blazh, Voronezh—voron, nozh!" ("Voronezh—whimsy, Voronezh—raven, knife!"). While Akhmatova's poem creates a similar ominous paronomasia from the city's name ("A nad Petrom voronezhskim—vorony"; "And above Peter-of-Voronezh—crows"), her Voronezh, perceived from a greater distance than Mandelstam's, is redolent of Russian history: the patterned sleighs, the statue of Peter who built a flotilla there, echoes of the nearby field of Kulikovo, where in 1380 the Tartars were defeated. The confidence of the image of the "slopes of the mighty, conquering earth" spills over into her triumphant vision of the poplars:

И тополя, как сдвинутые чаши,
Над нами сразу зазвенят сильней,
Как будто пьют за likованье наше
На брачном пире тысячи гостей.

And the poplars, like raised goblets,
Will all at once begin to ring out more strongly above us,
As if thousands of wedding guests
Were drinking to our triumph.

Yet the attempt to conjure reassuring images from the ice-bound city comes to an abrupt end in the final stanza:

> А в комнате опального поэта
>
> Дежурят страх и Муза в свой черед,
>
> И ночь идет,
>
> Которая не ведает рассвета.

> *But in the room of the banished poet,*
> *Fear and the Muse take turns standing guard,*
> *And a night comes,*
> *Which knows no dawn.*

The crowded wedding feast gives way before the lonely room with its three actors: banished poet, Muse, and fear. The sense of historical continuity the poem has developed is negated by the futureless night of the poet's fate. Reading backward to the poem's opening lines:

> И город весь стоит оледенелый.
>
> Как под стеклом деревья, стены, снег.

> *And the city stands all turned to ice.*
> *As if under glass, trees, walls, snow.*

—they become symbolic of the poet's "inaccessibility" in his frozen city of exile and, as Akhmatova foresaw, approaching death.

Mandelstam's fate shaped Akhmatova's image not only of the city of his exile but of his native city as well. In a 1937 poem to him, "Nemnogo geografii" ("A Little Geography"),[8] the city

> воспетый первым поэтом,
>
> Нами грешными — и тобой.

> . . . *glorified by the first poet,*
> *Us sinners—and you.*

is perceived as a place of exile and imprisonment:

Не столицею европейской
С первым призом за красоту —
Душной ссылкою енисейской,
Пересадкою на Читу,
На Ишим, на Иргиз безводный,
На прославленный Акбасар,
Пересылкою в лагерь Свободный,
В трупный запах прогнивших нар, —
Показался мне город этот
Этой полночью голубой,

Not a European capital
With first prize for beauty—
But a stifling Enisei exile,
A transfer at Chita,
To Ishim, to waterless Irgiz.
To famed Akbasar,
A transport to Camp Freedom,
To the corpse smell of rotting plank beds—
This city seemed to me
On this blue midnight,

Once more Akhmatova's Petersburg undergoes the transformation observed in the 1914 poem "That August, like a yellow flame," as well as in Akhmatova's memoirs of the city in 1920, into "the opposite of itself." The transformation in this case, however, is all the more frightening for having no "physical" basis, as did the previous cities transformed by war. The metamorphosis of the beautiful European capital into the Asiatic hell is based upon the perception of an "invisible" geography, in which Leningrad's true status within the Stalinist system becomes apparent.

Living in a city which for thousands, in point of fact, became a "transfer point" to Siberian imprisonment, Akhmatova, who was spared, experienced this freedom as both exile and imprisonment. In "Cherepki" ("Shards"),[9] which takes as its epigraph a line from James Joyce ("You cannot leave your mother an orphan"), Leningrad is the indifferent exile which, even in death, separates her from her son:

> Над моей Ленинградской могилой
> Равнодушная бродит весна.

> *Above my Leningrad grave*
> *Indifferent spring wanders.*

And in "Vse ushli, i nikto ne vernulsia" ("All have gone, and no one has returned")[10] as the one who has not been arrested, she speaks of herself as "the city madwoman" who wanders through the "death-bound squares" ("predsmertnye ploshchadi").

But the most developed and memorable picture of the prison city of the 1930s is, of course, *Requiem*, the "poema" composed between 1938 and 1940, which grew out of Akhmatova's personal tragedy. On March 10, 1938, her son, Lev Gumilyov, was rearrested. In essence, his only "crime" was his parentage: a father executed in 1921 as a counter-revolutionary, a mother existing on the fringe of Soviet literary respectability. Lev was imprisoned in Leningrad for seventeen months, but his death sentence was commuted to exile when those who had sentenced him were purged and shot. It was during the months of his Leningrad incarceration that *Requiem* was born, under circumstances vividly described by Haight:

> Akhmatova was terribly poor and living mainly on a diet of black bread and sugarless tea. She was extremely thin and frequently ill. She would get up from bed to go and stand, sometimes in freezing weather, in the long lines of people waiting outside the prisons, hoping against hope to be able to see her son or at least to pass over a parcel. When she was ill, friends would sometimes stand in the queue for her. The poems of "Requiem" composed at this time, were learnt by heart by

Lidiya Chukovskaya, Nadezhda Mandel'shtam and several other friends who did not know who else was preserving them. Sometimes Akhmatova showed them a poem on a piece of paper which she burnt as soon as she was sure it was committed to memory, sometimes she just recited them. Chukovskaya remembers going out late at night into the empty streets repeating a poem to herself over and over again, terrified she would forget a word or get something wrong.[11]

The enormous significance of *Requiem* to Chukovskaya, whose husband was executed, and to others like her, testifies to Akhmatova's success in transmuting her private experience into the universal one of those years. For *Requiem* records and memorializes a communal ordeal; Leningrad appears as a city of agonized, bereaved women, and Akhmatova is its voice.

In "Vmesto predisloviia" ("Instead of a Foreword"), which she appended to *Requiem* in 1957, she recalled:

В страшные годы ежовщины я провела семнадцать месяцев в тюремных очередях в Ленинграде. Как-то раз кто-то «опознал» меня. Тогда стоящая за мной женщина с голубыми губами, которая, конечно, никогда не слыхала моего имени, очнулась от свойственного нам всем оцепенения и спросила меня на ухо (там все говорили шепотом):

— А это вы можете описать?

И я сказала:

— Могу.

Тогда что-то вроде улыбки скользнуло по тому, что некогда было ее лицом.

In the terrible years of the Yezhov terror, I spent seventeen months on the lines outside the prisons of Leningrad. Somehow, once, someone "recognized" me. Then, a woman standing behind me, with blue lips,

who doubtless had never heard my name, stirred from the torpor which enveloped us all and whispered in my ear (there we all spoke in whispers):
—And can you describe *this*?
And I said:
—I can.
Then something like a smile passed over what had once been her face.

Akhmatova's description is dominated by two related impulses: to eternally preserve the memory of what occurred; and to distill from that experience its innermost spiritual significance. Although the actual number of lines devoted to the city are few, Leningrad is the "invisible" background of the poema as a whole. The room from which the husband is led,[12] the long-foreseen "bright day and abandoned house" where the speaker finds herself following the reading of her son's sentence, the room where she awaits her own death and struggles with madness—are in Leningrad.

The repeated assertion: "I was there, in Leningrad, at the place of crucifixion" is a strong unifying element of the poem, appearing both in the epigraph ("No, and not under strange skies") and in its epilogue. Comparison of this assertion of fidelity with that of the earlier poem "To My Fellow Citizens" reveals an essential difference. In 1923, Akhmatova spoke of "the wild capital" ("dikaia stolitsa"); here, she employs a similar image:

Подымались как к обедне ранней,
По столице одичалой шли,
Там встречались, мертвых бездыханней,
Солнце ниже и Нева туманней,
А надежда все поет вдали.

We rose as if for early mass,
Went through the city gone wild,
There we met, more breathless than the dead,

The sun was lower, the Neva mistier,
And hope still sang in the distance.

But whereas the "wild capital" of the 1923 poem is juxtaposed
with an eternal city of "palaces, fire, and water" which its cit-
izens suffer to preserve, the city of the thirties has no ar-
chitecture, no identity other than its prisons; it has been
rendered wholly impotent:

И ненужным привеском болтался
Возле тюрем своих Ленинград.

And like an unnecessary pendant
Leningrad dangled outside its prisons.

On one level, then, to be present in Leningrad is to par-
take of the shameful passivity of the Soviet city, through
which regiments of the condemned march toward the trains
which will bear them to their doom. Leningrad is not iden-
tified with the executioner; its sin, rather, is one of omis-
sion: it fails to provide either spiritual refuge or resistance to
the scourge.

For these, Akhmatova turns elsewhere, to a traditional
image of Russia itself:

Звезды смерти стояли над нами,
И безвинная корчилась Русь
Под кровавыми сапогами
И под шинами черных марусь.

The stars of death stood above us,
And innocent Rus writhed
Beneath bloody boots
And the tires of Black Marias.

Akhmatova's "innocent Rus" is a variant on "holy Rus"
("sviataia Rus'"), the pre-Petrine, Eastern Orthodox Mother

Russia, sacred to nineteenth-century Slavophiles. It is the suffering aspect of this Russia which Akhmatova emphasizes as she attempts to link her country's past and present cruelties. In the fate of the Streltsy[13] she finds a paradigm of Russian women mourning husbands destroyed by a dictator's ruthlessness:

> Буду я, как стрелецкие женки,
> Под кремлевскими башнями выть.

> *Like the wives of the Streltsy,*
> *I will howl by the Kremlin towers.*

But tracing the heritage of suffering is not enough; the anguish must be endowed with a redeeming significance. In superimposing the image of the Crucifixion upon Russia's sufferings, Akhmatova returns the impotent prison city to holy ground. She does so, almost imperceptibly, by forcing the reader to understand the name of the old Leningrad prison, "Crosses" (so designated because of its layout), in the original sense of the word:

> Показать бы тебе, насмешнице
> И любимице всех друзей,
> Царскосельской веселой грешнице,
> Что случится с жизнью твоей —
> Как трехсотая, с передачею,
> Под Крестами будешь стоять
> И своей слезою горячею
> Новогодний лед прожигать.
> Там тюремный тополь качается,
> И ни звука — а сколько там
> Неповинных жизней кончается...

> *They should have shown you, mocker*
> *And favorite of all your friends,*
> *Gay sinner of Tsarskoe Selo,*

What would happen to your life—
How, three hundredth in line with your parcel,
Beneath Crosses you would stand
And with your burning tear
Set fire to the new year ice.
There the prison poplar sways,
There's not a sound—but how many
Innocent lives are ending there . . .

As Leningrad becomes Calvary, Akhmatova rewrites the history of her personal relationship to the city. In her 1914 poem "The dark city on the terrible river," she had defined the city's legacy to her as a blessed cradle, sacred marriage bed, altar of her prayers, and place of first love and poetry. Here the worthiness of this Petersburg inheritance is replaced by the vision of a frivolous Tsarskoe Selo youth, perceived as ironic prelude to what was to come. The anonymity of her suffering as "three hundredth in line" is a denial of the inflated individuality of her early years. Yet in the very same image, she raises a new vision of personal dignity: the stature of one who stands before the Cross. She is simultaneously a victim of the twentieth century's mass horrors and the sublime figure of Mary. Cast in bronze and placed at the site of her torments, it is this eternally remembering and grieving figure which she offers as her own legacy to the city.

А если когда-нибудь в этой стране
Воздвигнуть задумают памятник мне,

Согласье на это даю торжество,
Но только с условьем — не ставить его

Ни около моря, где я родилась:
Последняя с морем разорвана связь,

Ни в царском саду у заветного пня,
Где тень безутешная ищет меня,

А здесь, где стояла я триста часов
И где для меня не открыли засов.

And if ever in this country
They think of raising a monument to me,

I consent to this triumph,
But only on condition that it be built

Neither near the sea, where I was born:
My last link with the sea has been broken,

Nor in the garden of Tsarskoe Selo near the sacred tree stump,
Where an inconsolable shade looks for me,

But here, where I stood for 300 hours
And where the bolts were not opened for me.

In her 1913 "Verses about Petersburg," Akhmatova framed the future of her "free" lovers between the "dark-watered Neva" and the "cold smile of the Emperor Peter." *Requiem* is similarly framed by concluding images of a bronze statue and the Neva. Yet the earlier "classical" images have been transformed: the indifferent statue has been replaced by a compassionate, grieving one; the darkness of the Neva's waters, binding past, present, and future, is given historic concreteness in the continuity of ships moving slowly along the Neva, forever accompanied by the cooing of the prison dove:

И пусть с неподвижных и бронзовых век
Как слезы струится подтаявший снег,

И голубь тюремный пусть гулит вдали,
И тихо идут по Неве корабли.

And may the melting snow flow like tears
From my motionless and bronze eyelids,

And the prison dove coo in the distance,
And ships go slowly along the Neva.

Thus is Akhmatova's Leningrad of the 1930s locked into its recent sufferings. The heroism of preserving the "stern but proud" Petersburg tradition is here overshadowed by the "podvig" (spiritual feat) of remembering injustice and suffering. For the moment, "Peter's holy temple" is neither a value to be preserved and defended nor a source of strength and protection against the evils of the age. Mary's sorrowful image replaces the commanding statue of Peter. Christ's Passion seems a more relevant myth for the times than the emperor's Promethean feat, that theft of fire from which a culture grew.

When Akhmatova does evoke the city's tradition, in the single Petersburg "love poem" of the thirties, "Godovshchinu posledniuiu prazdnui—" ("Celebrate the last anniversary," I/237, 1938), she brings the dark moments of its prerevolutionary history into intimate relationship with the grim present. Although it is a snowy night of their first "diamond" winter which is repeating, the lovers seem lost in the fog and darkness of the present:

Пар валит из-под царских конюшен,
Погружается Мойка во тьму,
Свет луны как нарочно притушен,
И куда мы идем — не пойму.

Smoke drifts from under the tsar's stables,[14]
The Moyka sinks into darkness,
The light of the moon seems purposely muted
And where we're going—I cannot know.

From the images which follow, it would seem that where they are going is backward—not to a personal past but to a public one:

Меж гробницами внука и деда
Заблудился взъерошенный сад.

> *Between the tombs of grandson and grandfather*
> *The disheveled garden has gotten lost.*

Akhmatova is referring here to the church "Salvation on the Blood" ("Spas na krovi"), built on the spot where Alexander II was assassinated in 1881 and the Engineer's (Mikhaylovsky) Palace, where Paul I was assassinated in 1881. The Mikhaylovsky garden is located between them.[15] By using the words "grandson" and "grandfather" to refer to the two murdered tsars, Akhmatova calls attention not only to the familial heritage of violence but to her own familial connection with this past. Akhmatova makes the city's history intimately her own, and these dark "anniversaries" cast their shadow upon the "diamond" one she is attempting to celebrate. The garden, which is often a positive image in Akhmatova, an oasis of beauty expressive of nature's fidelity to itself, when all else in the city's life is disrupted (cf. "That August, like a yellow flame"), is here "disheveled" and as lost as the lovers themselves. The only source of light—the street lamps—is itself infected with images of death and imprisonment:

> Из тюремного вынырнув бреда,
> Фонари погребально горят.

> *Having emerged from a prison delirium,*
> *Street lamps burn funereally.*

In the penultimate stanza, the nightmarish atmosphere is carried forward in the image of the "terrible icebergs" of Mars Field[16] (corresponding to the speaker's "fear"), but a lighter, more delicate form of "cold" is embodied in the image of the Swan Canal lying in crystals (corresponding to her "gaiety"):

> В грозных айсбергах Марсово поле,
> И Лебяжья лежит в хрусталях...

Чья с моею сравняется доля,
Если в сердце веселье и страх.

Mars Field is covered by terrible icebergs,
And the Swan Canal lies in crystals . . .
Whose fate is comparable with mine,
If there is gaiety and fear in my heart.

In the final stanza, images of delicacy and "lightness" prevail: the lover's voice, like a wondrous bird trembling above her shoulder, the sudden ray of light, the snowy dust turning warmly silver. The disembodied voice of the lover, the use of the word "prakh" ("dust")—which also has the meaning of "the ashes of the dead"—bring into question the actual presence of the lover, who is exhorted to "celebrate the last anniversary." There is an apparently "unmotivated" leap between this sudden moment of illumination, the recapturing of the "diamond" winter, and the nightmarish city in which the speaker wanders. While images of her "fear" predominate, an unspoken layer of memory gives rise to that flaring of inextricable "gaiety" inherent in Akhmatova's Petersburg fate. As we shall see, the "irrationality" of this positive climax in a poem which strongly develops the city's negative significance will be repeated in *Poem without a Hero.*

The Eternal Home

The image of a "native city," a spiritual home, does not vanish from Akhmatova's poetry of the years of the Terror. At the same time that she was creating the "impotent" prison Leningrad of *Requiem* and beginning her most complex and many-sided "Petersburg Tale," Akhmatova also wrote her poem of Kitezh, "Putëm vsia zemli" ("The Way of All the Earth," I/242–246, 1940). But Kitezh, the "drowned" city, toward which the heroine struggles through the tragedies and wars of the twentieth century, is only Petersburg-Leningrad, in its timeless hypostasis, by another name. The equation of the two cities has been made by Antsiferov, who speaks of "the second Russian legend of a drowned city, Kitezh and Petersburg," [17] as well as by Merezhkovsky, who stresses the "ghostly" nature of both cities.

The essence of the Kitezh legend is the notion of a city exempted from the horrors of history through its "removal" to an invisible realm: "Kitezh, according to legend, was a city saved by prayer from the advance of the Tartars. Some say it was lifted up to the heavens and its reflection seen on a lake into which the enemy rushed to their death, others that like other legendary cities it sunk deep into the lake where its towers can be seen on days when the water is specially clear." [18]

Precisely this "exemption" was denied Petersburg-Leningrad, which appears in this poem in the lines:

Столицей распятой
Иду я домой.

Through the crucified capital
I go home.[19]

Just as the fellow citizens of Akhmatova's 1923 poem were obliged to pass through the hellish city of the historical present in order to attain their immortality in "Peter's sacred temple," the woman of Kitezh can only reach her eternal home by way of the "crucified capital." In making this analogy between Akhmatova's Kitezh and her earlier "sacred Petersburg," I do not mean to obscure the essential point that in 1940 Petersburg-Leningrad, degraded by its recent history, was no longer a viable image of that ideal in Akhmatova's poetry.

The Great Martyr

In March 1941, on the brink of war, Akhmatova drew a poetic sketch of the city, "Leningrad in March 1941" (I/247), in which she affirms its centrality to her life:

О, есть ли что на свете мне знакомей,
Чем шпилей блеск и отблеск этих вод!

Oh, is there anything on earth more familiar to me
Than the gleam of spires and the glimmer of these waters!

The intent of the poem seems to be to capture a particular moment of the city's life: the "sunny hours on the Menshikov House" (a reference to the inscription on that building, located on the Neva embankment on Vasilevsky Island).[20] Akhmatova presents neutral images: a steamship passing by, a darkening intersection, sparrows sitting on a wire. Her attitude toward these isolated aspects of the city does not emerge until the poem's final lines:

У наизусть затверженных прогулок
Соленый привкус — тоже не беда.

The salty aftertaste of strolls
Learned by heart—is also not a misfortune.

If Leningrad is only too familiar to the speaker, a place where she continually covers the same ground, the "salty aftertaste" of these apparently inescapable repetitions receives her restrained affection.

But the city's full resurrection in Akhmatova's pantheon of values would occur only after it had passed through the crucible of World War II. If the history of the 1930s had brought the city to its lowest ebb, the martyrdom of the early 1940s wholly redeemed it.

In September 1941, at the beginning of the two-and-one-half-year siege, in which, virtually cut off from the rest of the country, the city would lose one and a half million people as a result of the fighting, disease, and starvation, and more than 10,000 buildings would be partially or totally destroyed, Akhmatova was invited to give a radio speech to the women of Leningrad:

My dear fellow citizens, mothers, wives and sisters of Leningrad. It is more than a month since the enemy began trying to take our city and has been wounding it heavily. The city of Peter, the city of Lenin, the city of Pushkin, Dostoyevsky and Blok, this great city of culture and labour, is threatened by the enemy with shame and death. My heart, like those of all the women of Leningrad, sinks at the mere thought that our city, my city, could be destroyed. My whole life has been connected with Leningrad: in Leningrad I became a poet and Leningrad inspired and coloured my poetry. I, like all of you at this moment, live only in the unshakeable belief that Leningrad will never fall to the fascists. This belief is strengthened when I see the women of Leningrad simply and courageously defending the city and keeping up their normal way of life. . . .[21]

Akhmatova's attitude toward the city in her war poems, consisting primarily of the cycle "Veter voiny" ("Wind of War"), is straightforward and easily comprehensible in broad patriotic terms. In several of the poems, she speaks with the voice of a mother for whose child (or children) the city has become a place of sudden death. In the second poem of the cycle "Pervyi dal'noboinyi v Leningrade" ("First Bombardment in Leningrad," I/261, 1941), the ordinary life of the city is suddenly transformed by a "sound" which belongs to no recognizable sphere of experience:

> И в пестрой суете людской
> Все изменилось вдруг.
> Но это был не городской,
> Да и не сельский звук.

> *And in the motley hubbub of human life*
> *Everything suddenly changed.*
> *But that was not a city,*
> *No, and not a country sound.*

It is a hellish thing whose "indifference" has the most personal of consequences:

И не хотел смятенный слух
Поверить — по тому,
Как расширялся он и рос,
Как равнодушно гибель нес
Ребенку моему.

And confused hearing
Did not want to believe,
How it widened and grew bigger,
How indifferently it brought
Doom to my child.

As in *Requiem*, and in her World War I poems (cf. "Why, then, did I carry you," I/169, 1918), Akhmatova assumes the persona of the grieving mother, which now hovers over the besieged city. This maternal image exists on several levels. In "Nox," subtitled "The Statue 'Night' in the Summer Garden," (I/264, 1942), which alludes to the attempt of Leningraders to save the city's statues by burying them next to their pedestals, Akhmatova addresses the statue of Night as a "dear Daughter," whom she attempts to save as Night's "terrible sisters" pass over the city. In Part I of "Pamiati moego soseda, leningradskogo mal'chika Vali Smirnova" ("In Memory of My Neighbor, the Little Leningrad Boy, Valya Smirnov" I/263, 1942), she is the mother of *all* Leningrad's children whom she calls "Peter's orphans, my dear little children!" ("Piterskie siroty, Deton'ki moi!"), Peter being the colloquial name for Petersburg. In the second part of this poem, she addresses herself to the little boy, who was her neighbor in the House on the Fontanka (Fontannyi Dom) until her evacuation to Tashkent and who perished in the siege.[22] Akhmatova, who wrote the poem in Tashkent, imagines that the dead child continues to exist in the Leningrad house. The "high mountain" which separates her from him becomes more than a geographical designation of the distance between Leningrad and Tashkent; it symbolizes the mutual inaccessibility of the realms of life and death. At the same time, however, as she defines this barrier, she denies it:

Постучи кулачком — я открою.

Я тебе открывала всегда.

Я теперь за высокой горою,

За пустыней, за ветром и зноем,

Но тебя не предам никогда.

Knock with your little fist—I'll open.

I always opened to you.

I am now beyond a high mountain,

Beyond the desert, wind and scorching heat,

But I will never betray you.

One may speculate that Akhmatova, evacuated through the whim of a government which, having systematically persecuted her and her family for twenty years, suddenly designated her important enough to save, felt guilt at having abandoned the city to its sufferings. Certainly that sense of personal failure is present in the lines

Твоего я не слышала стона.

Хлеба ты у меня не просил.

I did not hear your moan.

You did not ask me for bread.

Yet the predominant thrust of this poem is not guilt but the assertion of a continuous Leningrad community of the living and the dead. In a reversal of the tradition of the "dark" waters of the Neva, the ideas of resurrection and purification are now associated with the river:

Принеси же мне горсточку чистой,
Нашей невской студеной воды,
И с головки твоей золотистой
Я кровавые смою следы.

Bring me a handful
Of our pure, frozen Neva water,
And from your little golden head
I will wash away the bloody traces.

The most direct expression of this concept of a Leningrad community "outside of time" is "A vy, moi druz'ia poslednego prizyva!" ("And you, my friends of the final summons!" I/264, 1942):

Рядами стройными выходят ленинградцы —
Живые с мертвыми: для славы мертвых нет.

In well-formed rows Leningraders emerge—
The living with the dead: for glory there are no dead.

What, we may ask, is the "glory" in whose sight there are no dead, the ideal in whose service living and dead stand together? "Wind of War" continually asserts Leningrad's survival, sometimes defiantly, sometimes prayerfully, sometimes as in "Ptitsy smerti v zenite stoiat" ("Birds of Death Stand on the Horizon," I/262, 1941), as Chukovskaya has remarked,[23] with the tenderness usually reserved for a beloved person rather than for a city:

Не шумите вокруг — он дышит,
Он живой еще, он все слышит:

Don't make noise—it/he is breathing,
It/he is still alive, it/he hears everything:

(In Russian, the masculine pronouns "it" (for "city") and "he" are identical.) And in section 2 of "Pobeda" ("Victory," "January 27, 1944," I/266) the "fantastic" (nebyvalyi) fate which Akhmatova associated with the city's resurrection in the postrevolutionary years ("A fantastic autumn," "All is plundered, betrayed, sold out") now astonishes the city itself:

> И в ночи январской беззвездной,
> Сам дивясь небывалой судьбе,
> Возвращенный из смертной бездны,
> Ленинград салютует себе.

> *And in the starless January night,*
> *Itself amazed at its fantastic fate,*
> *Delivered from the fatal abyss,*
> *Leningrad salutes itself.*

Leningrad's resurrection has, on one level, of course, the very concrete meaning of national survival, the return to normal life of the starved, bombarded city. But there is another concept of survival for which its citizens fight and which erases the barrier between living and dead. In the most famous poem of the cycle, "Muzhestvo" ("Courage," I/262, 1942), Akhmatova speaks for her "fellow citizens'" readiness to preserve what is most precious; but here, in contrast to the 1923 poem, where self-sacrifice was in the name of "Peter's sacred temple," Akhmatova asserts:

> И мы сохраним тебя, русская речь,
> Великое русское слово.

> *And we will preserve you, Russian speech,*
> *The great Russian word.*

Amid the otherwise traditional rhetoric of this poem, this concept stands out as Akhmatova's unique brand of patriotism. Although Petersburg-Leningrad is not present by name in this poem, as the place of the communal struggle evoked by the cycle as a whole and the symbol of the Russian homeland, it is strongly implied. Thus, I would suggest, for Akhmatova, as for Mandelstam, faith in the city's endurance in time, and outside of time, is bound up with its role as repository of "the great Russian word," the "senseless, blessed word" of poetry, of which Mandelstam wrote in "We will meet again in Petersburg."

The phoenixlike Leningrad which emerged from the war would exist on two distinct planes: a real city of saved children and victory parks and a spiritual community of the living and the dead, preservers of the word.

Tashkent and Leningrad

Between the opening and concluding poems of "Wind of War," the outset of war and its victorious conclusion, lay Akhmatova's two-and-one-half-year sojourn in Tashkent. She wrote of this period: "Until May 1944, I lived in Tashkent, hungry for news of Leningrad, of the front. Like other poets I often gave recitals in hospitals, read my poems to wounded soldiers. In Tashkent I learned for the first time what the shade of a tree and the sound of water can mean in the blazing heat. I also learnt the meaning of human kindness: in Tashkent I was ill both often and badly" (I/46).

Akhmatova's poetic transformation of her Tashkent years, in the cycle "Luna v zenite" ("Moon at the Horizon," I/268–273, 1942–44) and a number of individual lyrics, contains reflections of this longing for her lost European city. In "Iz tsikla 'Tashkentskie stranitsy'" ("From the cycle: 'Tashkent Pages,'" I/321, 1959) walking through the city at night, in the company of another East European[24] she exclaims:

То мог быть Стамбул или даже Багдад,
Но, увы! не Варшава, не Ленинград,
И горькое это несходство
Душило, как воздух сиротства.

> This could be Istanbul, or even Baghdad,
> But alas! neither Warsaw nor Leningrad,
> And this bitter lack of resemblance
> Stifled us, like the air of orphanhood.[25]

And in section 6 of "Moon at the Horizon," she notes

> Третью весну встречаю вдали
>   От Ленинграда.
> Третью? И кажется мне, она
>   Будет последней.

> I meet the third spring far
>   From Leningrad.
> The third? And it seems to me it
>   Will be the last.

In spite of this nagging awareness of Leningrad's absence, Akhmatova's attitude toward her Asian refuge is overwhelmingly positive. It is a legendary, sometimes biblical, ancient land of splendid, aromatic flowers, birds, pure waters, and multitudes of stars. Her sense of kinship with this land mounts as the "Moon at the Horizon" cycle progresses, from the repeated challenge: "Who will dare tell me that this is an evil foreign land?" "Who will dare tell me that here I'm in a foreign land?"—to the assertion "You, Asia, are the homeland of homelands!"

> Он прочен, мой азийский дом,
> И беспокоиться не надо...
> Еще приду. Цвети, ограда,
> Будь полон, чистый водоем.

> It is firm, my Asiatic home,
> And there's no need to be upset . . .

I'll come again. Flourish, barrier,
Be full, pure reservoir.

The luxuriant natural life of Tashkent is a blessed refuge from besieged Leningrad.

С грозных ли площадей Ленинграда
Иль с блаженных летейских полей
Ты прислал мне такую прохладу...?

Is it from the terrible squares of Leningrad
Or from the blessed Lethean fields
You sent me such a coolness . . . ?

she asks in a section of the cycle addressed to her close friend, Garshin, who had remained in Leningrad. "Terrible Leningrad" and "blessed Lethe" are contrasted in these lines but also linked as two immeasurably distant realms of death. The contrast "Tashkent/Leningrad," is yet another embodiment of Akhmatova's duality: the city outside time, the city of the historical moment. Distant from the immediacy of war, Tashkent appears as an exotic, sensually tangible, and intoxicating Kitezh. It was, however, to remain only an episode, a flowering oasis in her life and poetry, before her return to the historical city.

Notes

1. See Haight, *Akhmatova:*

Akhmatova said repeatedly that she had never stopped writing poetry. Yet during these years of revaluation she wrote few poems. Once she told Lidiya Chukovskaya that she did not write poetry for thirteen years while with Punin in Fontannyy Dom. But when critics abroad later suggested that there had

been a period of silence she was furious. It is likely that she felt
the battle against this "shameful" silence . . . was something
no one outside Russia could comprehend, and that the weight
and importance of a single poem written in the conditions of
the thirties could in no way be compared to that of one written
in easier days . . . [pp. 84–85]

2. Haight reports that Akhmatova felt happier and freer in
Moscow in the latter part of her life "for a complex of reasons, both
personal and to do with the persecution she had gone through"
(ibid., p. 160). A pervasive feeling of homelessness, which extended
to both Moscow and Leningrad, is reflected in this interchange of
September 12, 1959, with Lydia Chukovskaya:

—"You know, Lydia Korneevna, I have lost a settled way
of life. It's already been eight years. I'm not at home in Peter,
nor here [Moscow]."
—"Was it from the time you left the Fontanka?" I asked.
—"I don't know. I didn't notice when it happened. But it
happened." [Chukovskaya, *Zapiski*, 2:293]

3. Ibid., 1:20.
4. Lev Gumilyov and Nikolay Punin were arrested in 1935
and were released shortly thereafter. Lev was arrested again in 1938.
5. In 1316 the city of Florence invited Dante to return, but the
terms offered him were those generally reserved for pardoned crimi-
nals. Dante rejected the invitation, maintaining that he would never
return unless he were accorded full dignity and honor.
6. D.M. Segal, "Fragment semanticheskoi poetiki O. E. Man-
delstama," in *Russian Literature* 10/11 (1975), p. 141. In his excellent
discussion of Mandelstam's poem, Segal points out that the theme of
Italy and Russia, which runs through all of Mandelstam's work and
forms one of the structural principles of his poetry, was in the end
embodied in the actual fate of the poet, that is, Mandelstam's exile
as a parallel to Dante's: "Thus, Mandelstam's situation in the mid-
thirties actualized the Dantean theme, and both cities merge into
one, forming the 'archetype' of the native and accursed, desired and
inaccessible city of its exiled poet."
7. Haight, *Akhmatova*, p. 88.

8. *Pamiati Akhmatovoi* (Paris: YMCA Press, 1974), p. 11.

9. Ibid., pp. 15–16.

10. Ibid., p. 25.

11. Haight, *Akhmatova*, p. 98.

12. While the greater part of *Requiem* deals with the ordeal of the son's arrest, Akhmatova also alludes, in "Uvodili tebia na rassvete" ("They led you away at dawn"), a section of the poema written earlier than the rest, in 1935, to the arrest of her third "husband," Nikolay Punin. (Although they lived together for fifteen years, Akhmatova and Punin were never officially married.)

13. The Streltsy were the bodyguard organized by Ivan the Terrible ca. 1550 and defeated and disbanded by Peter the Great, who then established a regular army. Eight hundred Streltsy were executed by Peter in 1698.

14. "This refers to the former Stable Palace (Koniushennyi dvorets) in Stable Square in Leningrad, between the Moyka and Mars Field—which adjoins the Swan's Canal and the Summer Garden" (*Anna Akhmatova: Stikhotvoreniia i poemy*, Biblioteka poeta [Leningrad, 1976], p. 477).

15. Ibid.

16. Ibid. "Akhmatova linked with [the region of Mars Field] historical reminiscences of tsarist Petersburg ("two windows of the Mikhaylovsky Castle, which remained the same as in 1801, and it seemed that behind them they were murdering Paul") and a series of events from her personal biography ("All this—is my Leningrad") [in the] Manuscript Section of the M. E. Saltykov-Shchedrin State Public Library," p. 477.

17. Antsiferov, *Dusha Peterburga*, p. 96.

18. Haight, *Akhmatova*, p. 116.

19. "The 'crucified capital' through which the *I* is wandering 'homeward' is to be understood, we think, as the image of Petersburg-Leningrad, the degraded capital which had become cruelly disfigured in the historical nightmare of the thirties—the 'crucified' Leningrad which the poet had evoked in *Requiem*" (Verheul, *Theme of Time*, p. 150).

20. *Akhmatova: Stikhotvoreniia i poemy*, p. 480.

21. Quoted in O. Berggolts, *Govorit Leningrad* (*Leningrad Is Speaking*) (Leningrad, 1964), pp. 15–16. The translation is from Haight, *Akhmatova*, p. 122.

22. For an account of Akhmatova's relationship with the family of Valya Smirnov, see Chukovskaya, *Zapiski*, vol. 1.

23. Ibid., 2:371.

24. Polish artist Joseph Czapski. See Haight, *Akhmatova*, pp. 129–30, for an account of their meeting.

25. An earlier variant to the line about Leningrad reads: "No tol'ko ne prizrachnyi moi Leningrad" ("Only not my spectral Leningrad").

The Postwar City

*We began to talk about how wet, dark and gloomy it
was on the streets.*

*"Leningrad in general is unusually well-suited for
catastrophe," said Anna Andreevna. "This cold
river, with heavy clouds always above it, these
threatening sunsets, this operatic, frightful
moon. . . . Black water with yellow gleams of
light. . . . it's all frightful. I can't imagine how
catastrophes look in Moscow; there they haven't got
all that. . . ."*

  *—From a 1939 conversation
  with Lydia Chukovskaya*

IV

I want to go to the roses, to that one garden,
Where the best wrought-iron fences in the world stand.
Where the statues remember me as a young woman,
And I remember them beneath the Neva's water.

Upon her return to Leningrad in 1944, Akhmatova had yet to come to terms with the immensity of the city's recent sufferings. Her sense of the city's martyrdom and of a grief too great ever to be wholly assuaged are expressed in "Prichitanie" ("Lamentation," 1944):[1]

Ленинградскую беду

Руками не разведу,

Слезами не смою,

В земле не зарою.

За версту обойду

Ленинградскую беду.

Я не взглядом, не намеком,

Я не словом, не попреком, —

   Я земным поклоном

    В поле зеленом

    Помяну.

I cannot brush aside Leningrad's
Misfortune with my hands,
I cannot wash it away with my tears,
I cannot bury it in the ground.
I walk a mile
To avoid Leningrad's misfortune.
Not with a look, or by some hint,
Not by a word, or a reproach,—
   But with a low bow to the earth
    In the green field
    I pray for it.

Two years later, in a poem marking the "Vtoraia godovshchina" ("Second Anniversary," I/287, 1946) of her return, Akhmatova is still the city's inconsolable mourner:

Но мнится мне: в сорок четвертом,

И не в июня ль первый день,

Как на шелку возникла стертом

Твоя страдальческая тень.

Еще на всем печать лежала
Великих бед, недавних гроз, —
И я свой город увидала
Сквозь радугу последних слез.

But it seems to me: in '44,
And wasn't it the first day of June,
Your suffering shade emerged,
As on worn-out silk.

The stamp of great woes, of recent storms
Still lay on everything,—
And I saw my city
Through a rainbow of last tears.

For Akhmatova, the city's public tragedy was insepara-
ble from those of her personal life. The anniversary of her re-
turn to Leningrad was also that of the day on which she had
learned that Garshin ("my care and comfort in the bitterest of
years") had married a nurse during the siege. As personal
losses accumulate, so do the "anniversaries," "hours of re-
membrance," and "unforgettable dates" which she is fated to
observe on her Leningrad calendar. Like Bely's Petersburg,
whose streets have the peculiar quality of turning the figures
of passers-by into shadows, Akhmatova's city increasingly be-
comes a place of shadows. Remembrance of previous griefs
and anticipation of new ones become two sides of her recog-
nition of the city as a place of inescapable disaster:

Опять подошли «незабвенные даты»,
И нет среди них ни одной не проклятой.

Но самой проклятой восходит заря...
Я знаю: колотится сердце не зря —

Again the "unforgettable dates" have approached,
And there isn't one among them that isn't accursed.

But the dawn of the most accursed one is coming up . . .
I know: it's not for nothing my heart is pounding—
[I/315, 1944]

Akhmatova incarnates the approaching disaster in the mani-
festations of a storm breaking into her room in the House on
the Fontanka and in Petersburg's characteristic nemesis—
flood:

На прошлом я черный поставила крест,

Чего же ты хочешь, товарищ зюйд-вест,

Что ломятся в комнату липы и клены,

Гудит и бесчинствует табор зеленый

И к брюху мостов подкатила вода? —

И все как тогда, и все как тогда.

I have placed a black cross on the past,
Then what do you want, comrade south-wester,

Why do the lindens and maples break into the room,
Why does the green gypsy camp buzz and commit outrages

And why has the water rolled toward the belly of the bridges?—
And everything like then, and everything like then.

This haunting "then," which the poet does not explain, any
more than she makes explicit the meaning of the "unfor-
gettable dates," becomes expressive of the city's fateful
recurrences, the binding of past to future through an inescap-
able fate.

Like Shelley's immutable mutability, this frightening,
predictable recurrence of loss becomes an axis of stability in
Akhmatova's postwar poetic world. The transformation of the
city to which she returned must have been, in its way, as dev-
astating as that which she encountered in 1915, returning—
not to the old capital, Petersburg—but to Petrograd. Her re-

turn to the room at the House on the Fontanka in which she wrote, "Again the 'unforgettable dates' have approached," was another shattering encounter with absence. In a 1960 conversation with Chukovskaya, who related the horror of returning to her old Leningrad apartment and finding nothing changed, Akhmatova replied:

> —When, on the contrary, everything changes in beloved places . . . , it's also terrible. Perhaps more terrible. I returned, at last, from Tashkent, to my room, which I had seen so clearly from a distance of thousands of miles. But, it turned out, everything was different: the tables and cupboard burned. The room empty, bare. I assure you, this is even more terrible. Beloved places ought to remain exactly the way we remember them.[2]

Loopholes to the Past

The failure of beloved places to remain as she remembered them gave rise in her poetry to the notion of a "meeting more bitter than parting," as she would call it in her Tsarskoe Selo poem, "Gorodu Pushkina" ("To Pushkin's City," I/315, 1944). The totality of the destruction of her "little toy town," depriving her of "loopholes to the past"[3] permitted Akhmatova to mourn it directly and to swear her allegiance "even beyond Lethe" to its memory. Petersburg-Leningrad's case was more complex. Its surviving streets, monuments, buildings offered her those "loopholes" absent in Tsarskoe Selo. Yet no simple passage to the past was possible. Akhmatova's most profound exploration of this theme is to be found in her "Severnie elegii" ("Northern Elegies"), which she originally called "The Leningrad Elegies." The earlier title is particularly appropriate, for the city's image is central to Akhmatova's poetic discoveries in this cycle. This is true, not only in the first elegy ("Pre-history"), where she presents a detailed portrait of the Petersburg of the 1870s, but in the three remaining elegies as well.[4]

In his discussion of the "Northern Elegies," Zhirmunsky notes:

> A comparison inevitably rises in the mind with "Epic Motifs," Akhmatova's first experiment in this genre, where the metrical form of blank verse, suggested by Pushkin's elegiac meditations, first appears. But there, the young poet's past seems almost to be present for her; it is thoroughly poeticized and steeped in an atmosphere of lyrical sadness. Speaking in the words of the "Northern Elegies," it is "the first epoch" of "remembrances."[5]

In "Epic Motifs," remembering the recent past, Akhmatova evoked Petersburg as a fresh, wintry landscape of lost innocence. In "Pre-history," she evokes the Petersburg of the 1870s, a period she did not directly experience but which she apparently reconstructed from her impressions of the 1890s:

> The first (lowest) stratum for me is the Petersburg of the nineties. It was covered from head to foot in tasteless signs—underwear, corsets, hats, completely without verdure, without grass, without flowers, it marched to a drum beat, forever reminiscent of executions, in the good French language of the capital, in grandiose funeral processions and the great thoroughfares described by Mandelstam.[6]

In spite of the remoteness of these memories, Akhmatova recalls them with a degree of specificity which led her contemporary, Korney Chukovsky, to testify that "the very colouring of that epoch, its very aroma is conveyed in 'Pre-history' with the greatest accuracy."[7]

It would be difficult not to sense, in this evocation of old Petersburg, as in the memoirs and other "historical landscape painting" of the last quarter century of her life[8] the impulse to recover "lost time," to recapture the flavor of past epochs, for the sheer pleasure inherent in that repossession. Beyond this, of course, Akhmatova is attempting to define her "inheritance," the fateful prologue to her generation's experience; and she accomplishes this not so much through the "accuracy" of her observations as through her specific selection and combination of details.

Verheul has written extensively on the pervasively *literary* nature of Akhmatova's re-creation of the times: the centrality of the themes of literature and literary creation, as a force shaping the chaos of raw experience, and the importance of Dostoevsky as "not merely the 'historical,' but also the 'thematical' protagonist of the poem."[9] He summarizes Dostoevsky's presence in the poem as an "image of the author whose biography is closely and tragically connected with his age—there are specific references to Dostoevskij's Siberian imprisonment and to his mock-execution on the Semenovskij square—and who through the act of his literary creation transforms and transcends the chaos of historical time."[10]

In addition to Dostoevsky, Nekrasov and Saltykov are directly named, while allusions are made to Tolstoy's *Anna Karenina* and, indirectly, to Turgenev's *Fathers and Sons*.[11] From the opening words of the poem "Dostoevsky's Russia" Akhmatova urges the reader to view the old capital through the eyes of its literary artists. In speaking of "Dostoevsky's Russia" or the "walnut frames of mirrors amazed by Karenina-like beauty," she implies that these authors grasped essential realities of their times, which are now inextricably bound up with their names. But there is also the sense that these literary allusions are an attempt on the part of the speaker herself to give shape to the otherwise eccentric, chaotic, sometimes ominous quality of the remembered life of the epoch, that is, the "theme" of art's shaping power is "tested" as a constructive principle in the poem itself. The shifting registers of the speaker's voice establish a tension between "artistic vision" and seething reality:

Россия Достоевского. Луна
Почти на четверть скрыта колокольней.

Торгуют кабаки, летят пролетки,

Пятиэтажные растут громады

В Гороховой, у Знаменья, под Смольным.

Везде танцклассы, вывески менял,

А рядом: «Henriette», «Basile», «Andre»

И пышные гроба: «Шумилов старший.»

Dostoevsky's Russia. The moon
Is almost one-quarter hidden by the bell-tower.
Taverns thrive, cabbies fly by,
Five-story enormities grow up
On Gorokhavaya, near Znamenya, next to Smolny.
Everywhere there are dance classes, the signs of money changers.
And next to them: "Henriette," "Basile," "André"
And splendid graves: "Shumilov, Sr."

The summary, categorical "Dostoevsky's Russia" and the ciphered image immediately following, which, if Verheul is correct, describes the appearance of the moon, one-quarter hidden by the bell tower of the Vladimir church, as it would be seen from Dostoevsky's worktable in his house in Kuznechny Lane[12]—may be seen as the poet's attempt to impose a specific "vision" upon the subsequent fragmented images of the city's hectic commercial life. In his commentary upon these lines, Chukovsky perceives them as a reflection of the ills of an unchecked capitalism descending upon "semi-feudal Rus."[13] But if so, Akhmatova's anticapitalist protest in these lines is aesthetic before it is political. The tastelessness of which she spoke in the autobiographical writing quoted above thrusts itself into memory in a series of transient names, which contrast with the one enduring name of Dostoevsky.

The speaker then attempts to impose a more satisfying form upon this motley past:

Но впрочем, город мало изменился.

Не я одна, но и другие тоже

Заметили, что он подчас умеет

Казаться литографией старинной,
Не первоклассной, но вполне пристойной,
Семидесятых, кажется, годов.
        Особенно зимой, перед рассветом,
        Иль в сумерки — тогда за воротами
        Темнеет жесткий и прямой Литейный,
Еще не опозоренный модерном,

However, the city hasn't changed much.
Not only I but others, too,
Have noticed how at times
It can seem like an old lithograph,
Not first-class, but quite decent,
Of the seventies.
        Especially in winter, before dawn,
        Or at twilight—when behind the gates,
        Coarse, straight Liteyny grows dark,
        Still not befouled by modernism . . .

There is a modest, comforting familiarity in the speaker's voice as she compares the city with an old lithograph of its own past. But the attempt to merge the Petersburg of the 1870s with the city of the 1940s in the image of "Liteyny . . . still not befouled by modernism"—interjects the jarring notion of that intervening age, when the street *was* defaced by buildings in the so-called modern style, that is, the period beginning just before World War I.[14] But the definitive failure to create an unchanging city becomes clear only when the speaker's attempt to present Nekrasov and Saltykov as existing in the present leads to the realization of the dominant temporal theme of the elegies: the inability of discrete and distant time frames to accommodate one another:

И визави меня живут — Некрасов
И Салтыков... Обоим по доске
Мемориальной. О, как было б страшно
Им видеть эти доски! Прохожу.

And vis-à-vis me live Nekrasov
And Saltykov . . . Both on memorial
Plaques. How terrible it would be
For them to see these plaques! I walk on.

The speaker "walks past" the horror of this realization to Staraya Russa, the town where Dostoevsky was living at the time with which Akhmatova's poem deals and the setting of *The Brothers Karamazov*. Yet this place, transposed by the nineteenth-century novelist from life to art, withholds its secrets from her. Her closing realization "And I will no longer go to the Optina Monastery"—where Dostoevsky went in his later years and where he met the archetype for his Father Zosima—as Verheul has observed, condenses the notion of her identification with the past and her inability to recapture it.[15]

In the remainder of "Pre-history," Akhmatova abandons the attempt to make past and present meet. In her description of fashions and interiors, she returns to an imaginative reconstruction which touches the present only through the echo of childhood memories. The evocation of her biological mother, who bequeathed her a "useless goodness," is followed by that of her spiritual father, Dostoevsky, whose heritage, pages which smell of the place of execution, is a more relevant gift:

Полночь бьет.

Перо скрипит, и многие страницы
Семеновским припахивают плацем.

Midnight strikes.

The pen scratches and many pages
Reek of Semenovsky Square.

Thus in the final image preceding the entrance of the speaker's generation upon the scene of life, the generalized "Dostoevsky's Russia" has narrowed to a single, ominous Petersburg landmark.[16] The Leningrad of *Requiem*, reduced to a place of imprisonment and execution, here finds its connection with the past.

"Pre-history," then, contains a complex blueprint of Petersburg's seductive "loopholes to the past." The significance of the past epoch, "understood" and distilled in Dostoevsky's pages, redolent of the place of execution, forms a bridge to the experience of Akhmatova's generation. At the same time, the attempt to see the city as a timeless community, belonging to the artists who lived there and shaped its literary image, is frustrated by the imposition of time's invisible architecture upon the city's familiar outlines.

In the successive elegies, time's architecture progressively overshadows the material city. In the "Second Elegy," Akhmatova abandons the theme of social continuity and disjunction to the attempt to grasp the passing of private epochs. In so doing, she abandons the "objective" approach to the city and creates of it an existential, internal landscape, in which the city's simultaneous "strangeness" and horrifying familiarity embody the duality of the speaker's sense of her journey in time.

Так вот он — тот осенний пейзаж,
Которого я так всю жизнь боялась:
И небо — как пылающая бездна,
И звуки города — как с того света
Услышанные, чуждые навеки.
Как будто все, с чем я внутри себя
Всю жизнь боролась, получило жизнь
Отдельную и воплотилось в эти
Слепые стены, в этот черный сад...
А в ту минуту за плечом моим
Мой бывший дом еще следил за мною
Прищуренным, неблагосклонным оком,
Тем навсегда мне памятным окном.

There it is—that autumn landscape
I have so feared all my life.
And the sky—like a fiery abyss,
And the sounds of the city—overheard as if
From the other world, forever alien.

As if everything with which I have inwardly struggled
All my life had taken on a separate
Life and grown incarnate in these
Blind walls, in this black garden . . .
And at that moment behind my shoulder
My former house was still following me,
With squinting, malevolent eye,
That forever remembered window.

City and self grow indistinguishable, for if, as the poet openly states, the city is here the incarnation of long-resisted inner demons, Akhmatova's imagery also incorporates an opposite process: the speaker and her past take on the attribute of the "granite" city:

Пятнадцать лет — пятнадцатью веками
Гранитными как будто притворились,
Но и сама была я как гранит

Fifteen years—like fifteen granite centuries
Seemed to close shut.
But I myself was like granite

The "city" (granite) here becomes an attribute of inaccessible time: immovable, stern, hard—the negative designation for the time lived with the lover. But it also characterizes the heroine's "hardness" and immovability in her decision to leave. This assertion of granite realities, however, is followed by uncertainties: the speaker's need to reassure herself that "all this has happened many times, and not to me, to others, too," her uncertainty as to whether it is a blessing or a curse, and, "most terrible of all," her own voice out of the darkness reminding her of the first, blessed, day of union with the beloved and bitterly exhorting her to celebrate her silver anniversary.

The evocation of this joyous silver anniversary, which the speaker has missed, this "nonanniversary," leads directly into the description in the "Third Elegy" of "the life not lived." In his discussion of the poetic reality accorded to this "unlived life," Verheul notes: "The contrastive image of her life as it has become in reality receives less prominence, and it gradually almost completely recedes into the background of her thoughts. Only once it suddenly comes to the foreground in connection with the theme of the beloved city."[17]

О, сколько очертаний городов
Из глаз моих могли бы вызвать слезы,
А я один на свете город знаю
И ощупью его во сне найду...

Oh, how many cities' outlines
Might have brought tears to my eyes,
But there is just one city on earth I know
And could grope my way to in sleep . . .

Just as in the earlier poems, the fate of the "splendid granite city of glory and misfortune" was contrasted with a "simple life," here Petersburg-Leningrad's presence is contrasted with "the unlived life." The speaker makes no evaluative statement about the city: she only states its reality, its singularity, its intense familiarity to her. In this sense—of her undeniable identification with it—the city stands as a point of affirmation in her "displaced" life. And in the image of that "displaced" life—a river deflected from its natural course by the stern epoch—one can discern echoes of the Petersburg myth: the "unreal, unnatural" city built upon a river by the stern will of its creator.

If, in the exploration in the "Second Elegy" and the "Third Elegy" of the vicissitudes of self-identity through time, the city has provided images of self-recognition, in the "Fourth Elegy," with its systematic delineation of the epochs of loss, it does not play even that minimally reassuring role. The city's image is wholly replaced by time's architecture: the blessed arch of the first epoch of remembrance, the solitary house in the remote suburb of the second epoch, to which one forgets the road, in the third. Petersburg is only a name—and an unspoken one at that—which changes and, like everything else, becomes "alien":

Но тикают часы, весна сменяет

Одна другую, розовеет небо,

Меняются названья городов,

But clocks tick, one spring replaces
Another, the sky grows pink,
The names of cities change . . .

The 1950s and 1960s: Invisible Victories

In the "Fourth Elegy," Akhmatova looks with unsparing clarity at the indifferent victory of time. Memory, the sacred principle by which she bound herself to the sufferings of her contemporaries, the victims of the Terror and the war, is here revealed in its impotence; it may keep faith, but it cannot keep alive the connection with the lost beloved.

Juxtaposed with this point of view are poems of the 1950s and 1960s which reveal an opposing strain of spiritual idealism: the assertion of a form of survival and communication outside time. A central expression of this spiritual realm is the cycle "Shipovnik tsvetët" ("The Sweetbrier Blooms"), dedicated to Sir Isaiah Berlin, whose 1946 meeting with Akhmatova, in the House on the Fontanka, led to disastrous consequences both for her and for her son, Lev.[18]

"The Sweetbrier Blooms" represents the final stage of the Petersburg love poems. In "Ty vydumal menia. Takoi na svete net" ("You invented me. There's no such one on earth," I/292, 1956), we find a recurrence of the early motif of the lover who miraculously comes to her door, having entered the city from an outer place. Akhmatova re-creates the setting for the lover's arrival, in postwar Leningrad:

Мы встретились с тобой в невероятный год,

Когда уже иссякли мира силы,

Все было в трауре, все никло от невзгод,

И были свежи лишь могилы.
Без фонарей как смоль был черен невский вал,
Глухая ночь вокруг стеной стояла...
Так вот когда тебя мой голос вызывал!

We met in an improbable year,
When the world's strength was already drained,
Everything was in mourning, everything bent with misfortune,
And only the graves were fresh.
Without streetlamps, the Neva's wave was as black as tar,
Dense night stood around like a wall . . .
That was when my voice summoned you!

The city in this poem and in the following one, "Nepopravimye slova" ("Irreparable words," I/292, 1956), is a timeless landscape of war's destruction:

И город, смертно обессилен,
Был Трои в этот час древней.

And the city, mortally weakened,
Was at that hour more ancient than Troy.

This is the apocalyptic devastation in which, more than thirty years earlier, following the destruction of war and revolution ("All is plundered, betrayed, sold out"), Akhmatova had discerned the seeds of a miraculous "coming." A similar expectation is suggested in "You invented me," where, in the midst of the city of darkness and death, the lover's arrival, which is both willed by the heroine herself and fated by some outer force, appears as a promise of new life:

Что делала — сама еще не понимала.
И ты пришел ко мне, как бы звездой ведом,
По осени трагической ступая,
В тот навсегда опустошенный дом,
Откуда унеслась стихов сожженных стая.

What I was doing—I myself still did not understand.
And you came to me, as if led by a star,
Walking through that tragic autumn,
To that forever abandoned house,
From which a flock of burnt poems had flown.

But the beginning of the poem, in which the heroine speaks of herself as nonexistent, and the cycle as a whole, belie the notion of resurrection in the usual sense.

In her earlier evocation of the meeting, "Naiavu" ("Awake," I/289, 1946), she juxtaposed a sense of "timelessness" and "placelessness" with the perceived quality of a white night. Similarly, as she creates the triumphant images of those non-meetings, following upon this first meeting, which was also the last, Petersburg-Leningrad turns into a nonplace, the very image of disembodiment:

И время прочь, и пространство прочь,
Я все разглядела сквозь белую ночь:

And time is gone, and space is gone,
I discerned everything through a white night:

In "Verses about Petersburg," Akhmatova consoled herself for the loss of a love affair by identifying it with the eternal life of the city in which it had taken place. "The Sweetbrier Blooms" makes a very different assertion of spiritual survival, one which is unconnected with the city as a cultural-historical continuum. If there is anything in the Petersburg tradition which suits it for the role Akhmatova assigns it in this cycle, it is the notion of the spectral city, Bely's Petersburg, in which the "shadow" and material worlds exist on an equal plane. In her unique development of this theme, Petersburg becomes "the looking-glass world of the *zazerkal'e*, a world which is more than a mere reflection, and which has a mysterious independent quality of its own."[19]

Gardens of Memory

Leningrad was beautiful that summer. I'm used to it,
I've seen it in every guise, but never like that. Cov-
ered in roses and poppies. The Summer Garden was
magnificent. But what a procession of shadows
follows me there. . . .

> —From a 1953 conversation
> with Lydia Chukovskaya

Thus in her later poetry, "this world" is increasingly accompanied by an invisible "double"—the world "behind the mirror" of unrealized events or the shadow world of the past. But for Akhmatova, who considered herself an Acmeist until the end of her life,[20] the bridge to that invisible world is always the visible one. The real places of Petersburg did not vanish from her poetry during these years. In her early poetry ("Verses about Petersburg," "That voice, arguing with the great silence," "That August, like a yellow flame"), she wrote about the Summer Garden as a "mysterious" enclave of "shaped" nature, associated with the sacred moments of love, a place of the city's eternal rituals, faithful to itself, even in the midst of history's upheavals, when the rest of the city has turned into "the opposite of itself." In the 1959 poem "Letnii sad" ("The Summer Garden," I/319) she returns to this theme, developing previous imagery into a full-scale evocation of one of Petersburg's sacred places. The theme of dual worlds is tranquilly contained within a unifying reality: the superlative wrought-iron fences of "that one garden":

> Я к розам хочу, в тот единственный сад,
> Где лучшая в мире стоит из оград,

> *I want to go to the roses, to that one garden,*
> *Where the best wrought-iron fences in the world stand . . .*

The Garden has now become a repository of her personal history, where she finds those reassuring "witnesses of events" whose loss, in the "Fourth Elegy," signifies a nightmarish estrangement from the past. Just as she addressed the statue *Night* as "dear little daughter" in the wartime poem, here she perceives the Garden's statues as girlfriends of her youth:

> Где статуи помнят меня молодой,
> А я их под невскою помню водой.

> *Where the statues remember me as a young woman,*
> *And I remember them beneath the Neva's water.*

The statues remember her beneath the waters of time; she them beneath the waters of the 1924 flood. Perhaps the proximity of the Summer Garden to the Neva, or more generally, the city's reflection in its river and canals, underlies the watery nature of the invisible world here. In this poem about the unseen, it is not the lindens (cf. I/194: "And the lindens were still green / In the mysterious Summer Garden") that she evokes but the silence between them:

> В душистой тиши между царственных лип
> Мне мачт корабельных мерещится скрип.

> *In the aromatic quiet between the royal lindens*
> *I seem to hear the creak of ship masts.*

There is, perhaps, a reminiscence in these lines of Mandelstam's "Nashedshii podkovu" ("He who found a horseshoe"):

> Глядим на лес и говорим:
> Вот лес корабельный, мачтовый,

> *We look at a forest and say:*
> *Here is a forest of ships, of masts,*

Mandelstam's own strong connection with the Summer Garden, as well as with Akhmatova's Petersburg past, would give him a prominent place in the procession of shades which are soon to follow. The lines of both poems suggest the unifying power of poetic imagination, of metaphor, which divines sound in silence, civilization (ships) in nature. Indeed, in the subsequent image of the swan which swims not through water but through time, Akhmatova's symbol of eternal beauty[21] is not a singular shape but a linking of one reality reflected in another:

> И лебедь, как прежде, плывет сквозь века,
> Любуясь красой своего двойника.

> *And a swan, as before, swims through the ages,*
> *Admiring the beauty of its double.*

Behind the imagistic dualities on which this poem is built, there is the underlying duality of life (the flowering life of the Garden, luxurious, recurrent; the eternal life of the statues; the speaker's own endurance) and death (the death of her youth, of past loves, of friends and enemies, whose shadows nonetheless go on living in the garden of memory):

> И замертво спят сотни тысяч шагов
> Врагов и друзей, друзей и врагов.

> А шествию теней не видно конца
> От вазы гранитной до двери дворца.

> Там шепчутся белые ночи мои
> О чьей-то высокой и тайной любви.

> *And in a dead faint sleep hundreds of thousands of steps taken by*
> *Enemies and friends, friends and enemies.*

> *And there is no end in view to the procession of shades*
> *From the granite vase to the door of the palace.*

There my white nights whisper
About somebody's lofty and secret love.

The reality of this Garden contradicts the ordinary, predictable nature of things: steps are immobile, shadows move, nights speak. In the concluding couplet, the Garden's dualities are bathed in a gemlike radiance; living and dead are illuminated by a single, "mysteriously hidden" source:

И все перламутром и яшмой горит,
Но света источник таинственно скрыт.

And everything burns like mother-of-pearl and jasper,
But the source of the light is mysteriously hidden.

Far less artistically convincing is another evocation of a "radiant garden" of those years "Primorskoi park Pobedy" ("Seaside Victory Park," I/297, 1950). As in "The Summer Garden," the poem's major theme is the victory over time and loss: the flowering of the new garden is both a memorial to the war dead and a symbol of resurrection. The essence of the city's founding myth: victory over formless, desolate nature, is retold. There is direct mention of Peter; but "Peter's time" is here an early stage of civilization, which the present era "corrects." Central to the poem is the idea of continual, victorious incursions of civilization upon wilderness; it is the planting of trees—as a symbol of civic memory—which creates this "radiant garden":

Но ранним утром вышли ленинградцы
бесчисленными толпами на взморье.
И каждый посадил по деревцу
на той косе, и топкой и пустынной,
на память о великом Дне Победы.

But early in the morning Leningraders
Came out in numberless crowds to the waterside

And each planted a young tree
On that spit, both swampy and deserted,
In memory of the great Day of Victory.

The opening scene of uninhabited desolation, and particularly the image of the "decrepit fishing boat," resonate with the opening lines of *The Bronze Horseman*. In addition to Pushkin, Lermontov's "Beleet parus odinokii, V tumane moria golubom" ("A solitary sail gleams whitely in the blue mist of the sea") is perhaps too obviously alluded to:

И там, где прежде парус одинокий
белел в серебряном тумане моря, —
десятки быстрокрылых, легких яхт
на воле тешатся...

And there, where formerly a solitary sail
Gleamed whitely in the silver mist of the sea,—
Dozens of swift-winged white yachts
Freely cavort . . .

The ease and absoluteness, evident in these lines, with which this victory is represented is perhaps the source of its artistic weakness. The radiant garden lacks a necessary shadowing; even its "watery double" is no more than a complacent reproduction of the original:

И вот сегодня — это светлый сад,
привольный, ясный, под огромным небом:
курчавятся и зацветают ветки,
жужжат шмели, и бабочки порхают,
и соком наливаются дубки,
а лиственницы нежные и липы
в спокойных водах тихого канала,
как в зеркале, любуются собой...

And now today—it is a radiant garden,
Free and spacious, clear, beneath the enormous sky:

Branches curl and flower,
Bumble bees hum and butterflies flutter,
And the young oaks flow with sap
And tender larches and lindens
In the peaceful waters of a quiet canal,
As in a mirror, admire themselves . . .

Those familiar with the continuity of Akhmatova's poetry recognize here an updated version, colored by patriotic optimism, of her fantasied "simple life"—and will feel uneasy about its placement within the boundaries of "the splendid granite city of fame and misfortune." The invisible victory of the Summer Garden is more persuasive.

The House of the Poet

Another image of spiritual survival connected with the city is Akhmatova's notion of "the house of the poet." She enunciated this, on an allegorical level, in "Antichnaia stranichka" ("Antique Page," I/324, 1961). In both parts, "Smert' Sofokla" ("The Death of Sophocles") and "Aleksandr u Fiv" ("Alexander at Thebes"), the destroying might of the political ruler is disarmed in the face of the unquestionable superiority of the spiritual man. The poet's house, the most valuable thing in the city, must not be destroyed:

Все, все предать огню! И царь перечислял
И башни, и врата, и храмы — чудо света,
Но вдруг задумался и, просветлев, сказал:
«Ты только присмотри, чтоб цел был Дом Поэта».

Everything, everything consign to the fire! And the tsar counted
The towers and gates and temples—wonder of the world,
But suddenly he fell to thinking and, brightening, said:
"Only take care that the House of the Poet remains whole."

If this ideal vision of power's respect for the spiritual man was the diametric opposite of the reality Akhmatova knew, in her own poetry she faithfully preserved the "houses" of poets. Just as she wrote, in *Poem without a Hero*, of her own inseparability from her city ("I am inseparable from you, My shadow is on your walls"), so in her poems she bound together the image of Petersburg-Leningrad and its great poets.

In the poem "Osipu Mandelstamu" ("To Osip Mandelstam," I/255, 1957) from the cycle "Tainy remesla" ("Secrets of the Craft"), she creates a "space" compounded of artistic, mythical, and actual Petersburg places which defines the poet's "pass to immortality":

О, как пряно дыханье гвоздики,
Мне когда-то приснившейся там;
Там, где кружатся Эвридики,
Бык Европу везет по волнам;
Там, где наши проносятся тени,
Над Невой, над Невой, над Невой;
Там, где плещет Нева о ступени, —
Это пропуск в бессмертие твой.

Oh, how spicy the breath of cloves,
I once dreamed of there;
There, where Euridices circle,
Where the bull carries Europa over the waves;
There, where our shades rush past,
Above the Neva, above the Neva, above the Neva;
There, where the Neva splashes against the step,—
Is your pass to immortality.

Zhirmunsky points out that the poem's mythological images may have been suggested by Akhmatova's artistic impressions of the prerevolutionary years: Gluck's opera *Orpheus*, staged by V. E. Meyerhold in 1911 at the Marinsky Theater, in which a chorus of Euridices circled on an underworld meadow, and the famous painting by V. A. Serov *The Rape of Europa* (1910).[22] He also notes, however, the appearance of these images in Mandelstam's poetry: "Chut' mertsaet prizrachnaia stsena" ("The ghostly stage barely glimmers) (which alludes to the Gluck opera) and "S rozovoi penoi ustalosti u miagkikh gub" ("With the rosy foam of tiredness at soft lips") I would add that the image of a "pass to immortality" may allude to a line from Mandelstam's "V Peterburge my soidemsia snova" ("We will meet again in Petersburg"):

Мне не надо пропуска ночного,
Часовых я не боюсь:
За блаженное бессмысленное слово
Я в ночи советской помолюсь.

I don't need a night pass,
I'm not afraid of sentries:
For the blessed, senseless word
I will pray in the Soviet night.

That Akhmatova has gathered the elements of *this* "pass" from the "blessed, senseless words" of Mandelstam's own poetry is further illustrated by the variant to this poem, which alludes to Mandelstam's "Eshche daleko mne do patriarkha" ("I'm still far from being a patriarch").[23] The insistence upon the image of the Neva is, of course, a tribute to Mandelstam's inseparability from his city, in both his life and poetry.[24] In the context of this poem, the Neva is both the living symbol of Mandelstam's immortality and the Lethe-Neva (an image Akhmatova first employed in her poem to Lozinsky ("Inscription on a Book," I/229, 1940) and developed in *Poem without a Hero*), the underworld river where the shades of both poets meet.

If Akhmatova's meeting with Mandelstam occurs in a complex space compounded of myth, art, and biography, her encounters with Blok,[25] in "Tri stikhotvoreniia" ("Three Poems," I/316–317), take place in "black memory." Mandelstam's Petersburg immortality is connected with the merging of classical and contemporary worlds; Blok's resides in his own figure—the central relevance of his poetic message to an understanding of the age:

И в памяти черной, пошарив, найдешь
До самого локтя перчатки,
И ночь Петербурга. И в сумраке лож
Тот запах и душный и сладкий.
И ветер с залива. А там, между строк,
Минуя и ахи и охи,
Тебе улыбнется презрительно Блок —
Трагический тенор эпохи.

And having fumbled in black memory you'll find
Gloves that come up to the elbow,
And the night of Petersburg. And in the twilight of theater boxes
That smell both sweet and suffocating.
And wind from the gulf. And there, between the lines,
Which omitted both "achs" and "ochs,"
There will smile at you, contemptuously, Blok,
The tragic tenor of the age.

As in her early poem about Blok, "Ia prishla k poetu v gosti" ("I came to visit the poet," I/115, 1914), Akhmatova associates him with the sea, "the gray and high house near the Neva sea-gates," which is reflected in his poetry. In the early poem, she focuses upon his eyes, perceiving in them something she would prefer to avoid:

У него глаза такие,
Что запомнить каждый должен;
Мне же лучше, осторожной,
В них и вовсе не глядеть.

He has the sort of eyes
That everyone must remember;
It would be better for me, cautious one,
Not to glance at them at all.

In her later memory of the poet, Akhmatova looks clearly at him, perceiving the contemptuous prophet "between the lines" of his tumultuous poetry. She says of him

Как памятник началу века,
Там этот человек стоит —

Like a monument to the beginning of the century
That man stands there—

In 1912, Blok wrote:

Ночь, улица, фонарь, аптека,
Бессмысленный и тусклый свет.
Живи еще хоть четверть века —
Все будет так. Исхода нет.

Умрешь — начнешь опять сначала
И повторится все, как встарь:
Ночь, ледяная рябь канала,
Аптека, улица, фонарь.

Night, street, streetlamp, drugstore,
A meaningless and dull light.
If you live another quarter-century—
It will still be that way. There's no way out.

You'll die—you'll begin again from the beginning,
And everything will repeat, as before:
Night, the icy ripple of a canal,
Drugstore, street, streetlamp.

Akhmatova assents to this grim vision of a repetitive, meaningless existence, the inescapable Petersburg decor:

Он прав — опять фонарь, аптека,
Нева, безмолвие, гранит...

He's right—again the streetlamp, drugstore,
Neva, silence, granite . . .

In the years in which these lines were written, Akhmatova was creating, in her *Poem without a Hero*, the fullest development of this theme of Blok's "rightness" and prophetic significance for his age. In that major oeuvre, she gathered not only Blok and Mandelstam but an entire artistic community under a roof broad enough to encompass the historical experience of her generation. Both outside time and trapped in the events of the "True Twentieth Century," the house bore the name of Petersburg.

Notes

1. *Pamiati Akhmatovoi*, p. 23.

2. Chukovskaya, *Zapiski*, 2:365.

3. The phrase is from Akhmatova's variant to "To Pushkin's City":

> Мой городок игрушечный сожгли,
> И в прошлое мне больше нет лазейки.

> *They have burned my little toy town,*
> *And I no longer have a loophole to the past.*

4. Cf. Zhirmunsky's note, pp. 506–07, in the *Biblioteka poeta* edition of Akhmatova's works for a history of the creation of the cycle.

5. V. M. Zhirmunsky, *Tvorchestvo Anny Akhmatovoi* (Leningrad, 1973), pp. 142–43.

6. Ibid., quoted on pp. 139–40, from Akhmatova's unpublished materials.

7. Korney Chukovsky, *Sobranie sochinenii* (Moscow, 1967), 5:741.

8. Other examples of Akhmatova's historical landscape painting are the Tsarskoe Selo poems: "Iunost'" ("Youth," I/276, 1940) and "Tsarskosel'skaia oda" ("A Tsarskoe Selo Ode," I/325, 1961) and the Petersburg poems "Peterburg v 1913 godu" ("Petersburg in 1913," I/326, 1961) and "Na Smolenskom kladbishche" ("At the Smolensk Cemetery," *Akhmatova: Stikhotvoreniia i poemy*, pp. 327–28, 1942). Akhmatova's interest in recapturing the precise details of pre-Revolutionary Petersburg life is reflected in this conversation with Lydia Chukovskaya, apropos of an article about old Petersburg by Lev Uspensky, published in *Zvezda* in 1957.

—"He writes that in old Petersburg the stairways smelled of coffee. What nonsense. The back staircases smelled of cats and the main staircases smelled of women's perfumes and men's cigars. . . . If it had smelled of coffee there, the master and mistress would have dismissed the hall-porter. . . . Then he says that in the evenings the faces of the women, under black or green veils, seemed full of mystery. . . . In the evenings, only prostitutes went out wearing veils." [Chukovskaya, *Zapiski*, 2:205]

9. Verheul, *Theme of Time*, p. 172.

10. Ibid., p. 174.

11. "There are some passing references to Tolstoy's *Anna Karenina* and to Turgenev in the phrase *Otcy i dedy neponjatny*, in which the title of his most famous novel is hinted at with a slight distortion of the original words" (ibid., p. 172).

12. Ibid.

13. Chukovsky, "Anna Akhmatova," p. 740.

14. *Akhmatova: Stikhotvoreniia i poemy*, p. 507.

15. Verheul, *Theme of Time*, p. 173.

16. *Akhmatova: Stikhotvoreniia i poemy*: "In a manuscript draft, dedicated to old Petersburg, among the terrible places, preserved in memory since youth, Akhmatova recalls 'Semenovsky barracks and Semenovsky Square, where Dostoevsky awaited death' and 'the gates from which they led members of Will of the People'" (p. 507).

17. Verheul, *Theme of Time*, pp. 178–79.

18. Akhmatova attributed both her son's arrest and her own denunciation by Zhdanov in 1946 to her meeting with Berlin. Cf. Berlin's account of this meeting in his *Personal Impressions* (London: Hogarth Press, 1980).

19. Verheul, *Theme of Time*, p. 201.

20. Chukovskaya in *Zapiski*, 2:417, quotes Akhmatova's statement on this theme, which was spurred by her frustration at the lack of comprehension with which six people read her *Poem without a Hero*: "And I'm an Acmeist, not a Symbolist. I'm for clarity. The secret of poetry is in its inspiration ["okrylennost'"] and depth, not in the inability of the reader to understand the action."

21. Comparison with Baudelaire's swan suggests itself ("Le Cygne"); yet Akhmatova's symbol of the purity of an earlier age is as graceful and serene as the French poet's is "ridiculous" and tormented:

Aussi devant ce Louvre une image m'opprime:
Je pense à mon grand cygne, avec ces gestes fous,
Comme les exilés, ridicule et sublime,
Et rongé d'un désir sans trêve! . . .

So, before the Louvre an image oppresses me:
I think of my great swan with his crazy motions,
Ridiculous and sublime, like exiles,
Relentlessly gnawed by desire! . . .

22. *Akhmatova: Stikhotvoreniia i poemy*, p. 482.
23. Akhmatova's lines

Это ключики от квартиры,
О которой теперь ни гу-гу...

It's the keys from an apartment
About which there's now not a peep . . .

refer to Mandelstam's lines

Когда подумаешь, чем связан с миром,
То сам себе не веришь: ерунда!
Полночный ключик от чужой квартиры,

When you think what connects you to the world,
You don't even believe yourself: nonsense!
A midnight key to a strange apartment,

24. For a full-length study of Mandelstam's Petersburg, see my unpublished doctoral dissertation, "The City Visions of Osip Mandel'štam" (Ann Arbor: University of Michigan, 1976). Also see my article "Mandel'štam's Petersburg: Early Poems of the City Dweller," *Slavic and East European Journal*, vol. 22, no. 4 (1978), pp. 473–83.

25. See Zhirmunsky's "Anna Akhmatova i Aleksandr Blok," *Russkaia literatura*, no. 3 (1970), pp. 37–82.

Poem Without a Hero

It is terrifying to think that our life is a tale without a plot or a hero, made out of emptiness and glass, out of the fevered babble of constant digressions, out of Petersburg's influenzal delirium.

—*Osip Mandelstam*, Egipetskaia marka (The Egyptian Stamp)

Akhmatova and Olga Sudeykina, 1924

*A*khmatova created her most encompassing city, the many-layered Petersburg vision of *Poema bez geroia* (*Poem without a Hero*), not all at once, but in repeated spurts of building, demolition, and rebuilding, over a span of more than twenty years. She began the work in prewar Leningrad, in 1940, and did not consider it completed until 1962. In the 1955 "Iz pis'ma K.N." ("From a Letter to K.N."), which was deleted from the *Poema*'s final version, she describes the work's extraordinary hold on her: "and still for fifteen years this poem kept catching me unexpectedly, over and over, like fits of some incurable illness (it could happen anywhere—at concerts, while the music was playing, on the street, even in my dreams), and I could not tear loose from it, as I kept adding to and correcting an apparently completed work."

Both the length and obsessive nature of Akhmatova's involvement with the *Poema* suggest that, in writing it, she was searching for the elusive "answer to the riddle of my life," which she speaks of in chapter 3. More than any other single work of hers, it lays claim to being considered her poetic summary.

In the immense integrative task she set for herself, Petersburg was her central unifying symbol: the place where past, present, and future; living and dead; art, personal biography, and national destiny were to meet and intertwine. *Poem without a Hero* is, above all, "A Petersburg Tale." In giving part 1 this subtitle, the same that Pushkin gave to his *The Bronze Horseman*, Akhmatova places her work squarely in the tradition of the city's apocalyptic poems.

Like Pushkin's poem, Akhmatova's is structured upon the association of a Petersburg catastrophe with a tragic love story. In Pushkin, the clerk Evgeny loses his betrothed in the flood which engulfs the city. In Akhmatova's love story, the protagonists had actual prototypes: Vsevolod Knyazev, the young cornet and poet who, in 1913, unhappy in his love for Akhmatova's friend, the Petersburg beauty and actress Olga Sudeykina, took his own life. Akhmatova takes the kernel of this event, which occurred against the backdrop of another rising flood—the global war and revolution, which would sweep away the world of Akhmatova's youth—and makes of it a touchstone for grasping the meaning of that world, its ending, and its aftermath in the new Soviet era.

Literary Memory

*It is a strange thing, very strange. I always wrote
my poems by myself. But the* Poema *was different. I
wrote the whole of it as if in chorus with others
prompting.*
> —From a conversation with Lydia
> Chukovskaya, December 1955

*And as I did not have enough paper, I wrote on your
first draft. And here one of the words came through.*
> —First Dedication, Poema bez geroia[1]

In the "tumulus of learned commentary . . . inexorably rising over"[2] Akhmatova's most difficult and "encoded" work, much energy and erudition has been devoted to uncovering the numerous allusions and quotations from the work of other writers, the presence of which Akhmatova anticipated would earn her the accusation of plagiarism.[3] One of the earliest "investigators" of this aspect of Akhmatova's work was Nadezhda Mandelstam who, after hearing Akhmatova recite the *Poema* for the first time, in Tashkent, asked her to whom the first dedication was addressed. She received the irritated reply: "Whose first draft do you think I can write on?"[4] implying, of course, that Mandelstam's "first draft" was the crucial one. The title of the work, which is taken from Mandelstam's *Egipetskaia marka* (*The Egyptian Stamp*),[5] the date of the first dedication, "January 27, 1940," which corresponds to the date of Mandelstam's death, two years earlier,[6] the reference to Antinous's dark lashes, a physical characteristic which

Akhmatova strongly associated with Mandelstam,[7] the direct quotation of Mandelstam's words to Akhmatova, reported in her memoirs of him, "I am ready to die," as well as Mandelstam's indisputable "right to such esteem for [his] first draft,"[8] as opposed to Knyazev, a minor poet[9]—all suggest that Mandelstam provided an important subtext for Akhmatova's work. Yet any attempt to ascribe the underlying "first draft" to a single writer will inevitably distort the work's polyphonic nature. The numerous "voices from the chorus" which scholars have already identified, include those of Pushkin, Lermontov, Gogol, Dostoevsky, Blok, Annensky, Kuzmin, Bely, and Mandelstam—to mention only the most prominent of the chorus's Russian members.[10] While the thematic significance of both the lives and the works of these writers to the *Poema*'s concerns has frequently been discussed, less attention has been devoted to the overall significance of the existence of this chorus for an understanding of the work's poetic thrust.

To a large extent, the *Poema* is "about" literature itself. "Reshka" ("Tails," as in the reverse side of a coin) consists of the poet's reflections upon the nature of the work she has written and its relationship to the nineteenth-century poema. "Vmesto predisloviia" ("In Place of a Foreword") and "From a letter to K.N." deal with the *Poema*'s "arrival" and its reception by its first readers. The intensity of Akhmatova's creative relationship with this work explains, on a psychological level, the amount of space which the *Poema* dedicates to contemplating its own image: "zerkalo zerkalu snitsia," in the *Poema*'s own words, "the mirror dreams of a mirror." Yet the question remains: how are the themes of literature and literary creation related to the *Poema* as an artistic whole?

My suggestion is that Akhmatova's literary "digressions" are central to the work's overall concept. On the one hand, literature is not an abstract concept but a living one. Akhmatova continually speaks of the *Poema* as a living being, or as a ghost come back to haunt her, or as a palpable object:

НУ, А ВДРУГ КАК ВЫРВЕТСЯ ТЕМА,
КУЛАКОМ В ОКНО ЗАСТУЧИТ, —

BUT WHAT IF SUDDENLY A THEME BREAKS THROUGH,
KNOCKS ON THE WINDOW WITH ITS FIST,—
["Afterword"]

И была для меня та тема,
   Как раздавленная хризантема
     На полу, когда гроб несут.

And for me that theme
   Was like a crushed chrysanthemum
     On the floor as a coffin is being carried out.
["Tails"]

А столетняя чаровница
   Вдруг очнулась и веселиться
     Захотела.

But the hundred-year-old enchantress
   Suddenly awoke and wanted
     To have some fun.
["Tails"]

On the other hand, Akhmatova's representation of "life" in the *Poema* is inseparable from the representation of life in literature. The extent to which Akhmatova's perception of reality, particularly in the postwar years, was filtered through the vision of the great literature of the past, is indicated by Berlin in his description of Akhmatova in 1945:

Leningrad after the war was for her nothing but a vast cemetery, the graveyard of her friends: it was like the aftermath of a forest fire—the few charred trees made the desolation still more complete. She had devoted friends . . .—but her sustenance came not from them but from literature and the images of the past: Pushkin's St. Petersburg; Byron's, Pushkin's, Mozart's, Molière's Don Juan; and the great panorama of the Italian Renaissance.[11]

If, as many have suggested, the impulse underlying the *Poema* is the resummoning of the Petersburg past, in N. Mandelstam's words "a last backward glance at the 'red towers' of her 'native Sodom'"[12] it is also a grand summing up of that city's literary tradition. Complementing the notion of memory as a sacred obligation to the past is the notion of *literary memory*. Akhmatova's masquerade, the "hellish harlequinade" of 1913, draws together not only the leading figures of the pre-revolutionary art world but a masked entourage of Petersburg's literary themes.

It is in this sense, perhaps, that Mandelstam is central to the *Poema*, in a way different from that of any of the other writers to whom it alludes. For Mandelstam, "writing in chorus," the direct and indirect quotation of other writers, was an omnipresent feature of his work, based on his belief in the eternal recurrence of the poetic word and in its ability to transcend barriers of time and language.[13] Mandelstam directly formulated the beliefs underlying the "Poesie der Poesie" aspect of his work,[14] his tendency to write as much about previous artistic visions of life as about life itself, in his 1914 poem "Ia ne slykhal rasskazov Ossiana" ("I didn't hear Ossian's tales"):

Я получил блаженное наследство —
Чужих певцов блуждающие сны;

I have received a blessed inheritance—
The wandering dreams of other poets

and in the famous words of "Tristia":

Все было встарь, все повторится снова,
И сладок нам лишь узнаванья миг.

Everything has been, everything will repeat,
And only the moment of recognition is sweet to us.

as well as in his essay "Slovo i kul'tura" ("The Word and Culture"): "Yesterday has not yet been born. It still has not authentically existed. I want Ovid, Pushkin and Catullus again and I am not satisfied with the historical Ovid, Pushkin, Catullus." [15]

In summoning back the Petersburg literary past, Akhmatova, too, is dissatisfied with "the historical Ovid, Pushkin, Catullus," that is, in rendering a final homage to a literary tradition, she does more than "remember"; she "respeaks" it. As her second epigraph to chapter 3, she quotes the first two lines of this stanza by Mandelstam:

В Петербурге мы сойдемся снова,
Словно солнце мы похоронили в нем,
И блаженное, бессмысленное слово
В первый раз произнесем.

In Petersburg, we will meet again,
As if we had buried the sun there,
And the blessed, senseless word
We will speak for the first time.

Poem without a Hero may be viewed as Akhmatova's attempt to fulfill this prediction: to "meet again" in Petersburg and speak the eternally recurring, eternally new word of poetry. It is Akhmatova's grand summation of previous literary Petersburgs, including her own; for she is writing on her own first draft, that is, on her own past evocations of the city, as well as on those of others. But it is also a transformation and unification of those diverse visions, through the unique perspective of her later years:

ИЗ ГОДА СОРОКОВОГО,
КАК С БАШНИ, НА ВСЕ ГЛЯЖУ.
КАК БУДТО ПРОЩАЮСЬ СНОВА
С ТЕМ, С ЧЕМ ДАВНО ПРОСТИЛАСЬ,
КАК БУДТО ПЕРЕКРЕСТИЛАСЬ
И ПОД ТЕМНЫЕ СВОДЫ СХОЖУ.

FROM THE YEAR NINETEEN-FORTY,
AS FROM A TOWER, I LOOK OVER ALL
AS IF I WERE PARTING AGAIN
WITH WHAT I LONG AGO SAID FAREWELL TO,
AS IF I HAD CROSSED MYSELF
AND WERE WALKING UNDER DARK VAULTS.
[*"Introduction"*]

This is a double perspective, implying both distance from (the tower) and continued participation in ("walking under dark vaults") the reality she describes. Of all those writers whose visions of the human condition, of Russia and history, were inseparable from and nourished by a vision of Petersburg, only Akhmatova was granted so long and fateful a perspective—from turn-of-the-century Petersburg to postwar and post-Stalinist Leningrad—and so intimate a participation in the city's history. In the "magical mirror" of the *Poema*, Petersburg themes born in the "fantastic city" in earlier times—Shadow, Mask, Devil, Double, Avenger—speak the language of the new era.

The Fantastic City Revisited

Akhmatova's evocation of the city relies heavily upon the image of that "fantastic Petersburg"[16] which, from Pushkin to Bely and Blok, has stood at the center of the city's myth. Her awareness of her indebtedness to this tradition is revealed in her notes to the *Poema*, in which she speaks of its link to the "Petersburg Hoffmaniana."[17] But the renowned genealogy of Akhmatova's fantastic city should not obscure the originality of her artistic conception. Her city of illusion is an expression of the great themes of her later years: an implacable sense of guilt bound up with the past; the relentless epochs of memory and forgetting, which forever separate the living from the dead; and the contrasting vision of a spiritual victory over fate, through a "historical community of the living and the dead." [18]

In the "Fourth Elegy," Akhmatova developed her concept of the gradual, implacable alienation of living and dead in the image of an isolated house to which we have forgotten the path; rushing there "in shame and anger," we discover that we have come to the wrong house:

Мы сознаем, что не могли б вместить
То прошлое в границы нашей жизни,
И нам оно почти что так же чуждо,
Как нашему соседу по квартире,

We realize that we could not fit that past
Within the boundaries of our lives,
And that it is almost as alien to us
As to the man in the apartment next door,

Yet this existential awareness coexisted with a persistent and powerful need for a moral confrontation with the past and with her own self in that past. How was she to reach that "isolated house in a remote suburb" where the dead managed so well without her?

The symbol of another house was to play a central role in creating this artistic confrontation. The number of Akhmatova's poems whose date lines are followed by the words "House on the Fontanka" ("Fontannyi Dom") already assured this late baroque building, the former palace of the Sheremetevs, of a distinct place in Russian literary history. But its place in the *Poema* transformed the House on the Fontanka from an element of Akhmatova's biography to a poetic symbol in its own right. As a Petersburg literary landmark it belongs, not with the great public monuments—the Statue of Peter, the Admiralty, Nevsky Prospect, St. Isaac's, the Summer Garden—but with the city's legendary inner space: the delirium-wracked rooms of the city's dreamers: Piskarëv's wretched studio, Akaky's meager lodging, Mr. Golyadkin's rooms on Shestilavochnaya St., Raskolnikov's room, Dudkin's room.

The symbolic meanings which the House on the Fontanka acquires in the *Poema* are closely related to the poet's biographical experiences. Akhmatova shared an apartment in this house with Nikolay Punin and his former wife and daughter for fifteen years; when she left him, she continued living in that apartment, merely exchanging rooms with the former wife, until her evacuation to Tashkent. She returned to this room after the blockade and remained there for many years. It was thus the house in which she had the longest single period of residence in all of her peripatetic life. It was one of her beloved places, home. At the same time, it was a house of tormented memories, the symbol of the failure of her relationship with Punin; returning to it after the war, she found her old room plundered, half-destroyed, filled with memories of the dead, a prototype for what Verheul has called "the house of the I, haunted by horrifying and generally unspecified events from the past." [19]

The dualities home/nonhome, identification/estrangement, and possession/loss are all present in the poetic "space" of the House on the Fontanka masquerade. The masked figures of the dead do not simply "visit" the house of the author, injecting their alien presence into a familiar ambience. The author meets them on the threshold of her house and undergoes traumatic, transforming sensations:

> Я сама, как тень на пороге,
> Стерегу последний уют.
> И я слышу звонок протяжный,
> И я чувствую холод влажный,
> Каменею, стыну, горю...

> *Like a shade on the threshold I myself*
> *Guard the final cozy refuge.*
> *And I hear a protracted ring at the door,*
> *And I feel a clammy cold,*
> *I turn to stone, I freeze, I burn . . .*

Just as the author herself becomes "something else" in the process of meeting her guests, so her house is transformed into another kind of space:

> И для них расступились стены,
> Вспыхнул свет, завыли сирены,
> И, как купол, вспух потолок.

> *And the walls moved apart for them,*
> *Lights flared on, sirens wailed,*
> *And the ceiling bulged like a cupola.*

The implied comparison of the transformed apartment with a church, inherent in the word "cupola," is in stark contrast to the flaring lights and sirens, the generally "hellish" atmosphere which surrounds the masquerade. This merged holy/unholy space is an expression of that ambivalent attitude toward the past she evokes which has been noted by virtually all commentators on the *Poema*.

Akhmatova has written that to view prerevolutionary Russia "from the heights of the mid-20th century without dizziness is almost impossible." [20] It follows, then, that dizziness, the "Petersburg delirium," is the only feasible medium for reaching that past. [21] The holy/unholy space of the House on the Fontanka is Akhmatova's artistic answer to the "isolated house in the remote suburb," a way of overcoming the mutual isolation of the living and the dead. But it is also a way of maintaining that isolation. The author does not confront the vivid, sensual reality of "the first epoch of remembrance," but instead of the progressive, devastating loss of the second and third epochs, she conjures a sweeping series of images, which embody, in highly encoded and compressed form, her sense of the past, as well as her overall vision of history.

In the masquerade of figures from the prerevolutionary era, which is the central "fantastic" event of the *Poema*, Akhmatova is drawing upon another facet of the tradition of the "city of illusion." [22] Lermontov's drama "Masquerade," with its vision of life as delusion, the fateful triangle of Arbenin, Nina, and the Prince, the picture of gay, empty society life whirling toward destruction—was doubtless a compelling model for Akhmatova's conception. The masquerade in Bely's *Petersburg* may have been an additional source for the *Poema*. [23] In Bely's city, where everyone is habitually masked, and the removal of one mask only reveals another, the masquerade scene, with its resulting revelations and false representations, is only a heightened occasion for the city's impenetrable chaos.

As in Bely and Lermontov, Akhmatova's masks whirl toward a doom, which is—here—both the historical cataclysm of the First World War and of the Bolshevik Revolution and a Last Judgment, which still awaits:

Но мне страшно: войду сама я,
   Кружевную шаль не снимая,
    Улыбнусь всем и замолчу.
С той, какою была когда-то,
   В ожерельи черных агатов,
    До долины Иосафата
     Снова встретиться не хочу...

But I am terrified: I myself will enter,
   Without removing my lacy shawl,
    I'll smile to everyone and be silent.
Before the Valley of Jehosaphat,
   I have no wish to meet again
    Myself as I once was,
     Wearing a necklace of black agates . . .

Having dressed herself in the famous "costume" of her youth, the shawl in which both Blok and Mandelstam memorialized her and the necklace of black agates in which she was painted,[24] Akhmatova evokes her own previous night city of "We are all drunkards here, harlots," with its aura of dissolution, sin, and retribution:

> О, как сердце мое тоскует!
> Не смертного ль часа жду?
> А та, что сейчас танцует,
> Непременно будет в аду.

> *O how my heart aches!*
> *Aren't I awaiting the final hour?*
> *And that woman who's dancing now*
> *Will surely go to hell.*

Both the artistic nightclub, "The Stray Dog," and Olga Sudeykina have been transported from this early impressionistic miniature into the convoluted space of the *Poema*, where Judgment is both past and still in the future. The masked figures of Akhmatova's Petersburg past have already met their doom, while she, who has been left behind in the world of the living, strives to reunite her fate with theirs.

She does this, in great measure, through the very nature of her "characterizations," central to which is the concept of "the double." Unable to encounter herself in the past, she encounters, instead, figures who embody the reality of that past, as well as the future which must inevitably follow. The figure she directly identifies as her double, in part 1, is, of course, the Sudeykina figure:

> ...Ты в Россию пришла ниоткуда,
> О мое белокурое чудо,
> Коломбина десятых годов:
> Что глядишь ты так смутно и зорко,

Петербургская кукла, актерка,

Ты — один из моих двойников.

К прочим титулам надо и этот

Приписать. О подруга поэтов,

Я наследница славы твоей.

. . . *To Russia you came out of nowhere,*

O my flaxen-haired miracle,

Columbine of the nineteen-tens:

Why do you stare so sadly and so sharply,

You Petersburg doll, you cheap actress—

You are one of my doubles.

To the others this title too

Must be added. O companion of poets,

I am heir to your fame.

The author clearly states the basis of her identification with Olga:[25]

Не сердись на меня, Голубка,

Что коснусь я этого кубка:

Не тебя, а себя казню.

Все равно подходит расплата —

Don't be angry at me, my Dove,

For touching this goblet too:

I'm punishing myself, not you.

No matter what, retribution draws near—

As in "We are all drunkards," it is the sense of sin and guilt for the frivolous carnival of their youth which Akhmatova shares with the Sudeykina figure. In the *Poema*, where the cornet's suicide is (at least in part) a symbol of the tragic wastefulness of those years, the fact that, in reality, Akhmatova may have been in love with Knyazev, who killed himself for love of Olga, is irrelevant. It is not necessary to seek, or to presume the existence of, a specific basis for guilt in the author's past, a "guilty secret," which, in Van der Eng-Liedmeier's formulation is implied but never specifically revealed to the reader. If this "hidden" theme of the author's personal guilt were, in fact, the "most important,"[26] then the complete silence surrounding it would constitute a serious shortcoming of the *Poema*.

In "Tails," where the author explores the nature of her creation, she states openly:

> Скоро мне нужна будет лира,
>   Но Софокла уже, не Шекспира.
>   На пороге стоит — Судьба.

> *Soon I will need a lyre,*
>   *But of Sophocles, not of Shakespeare.*
>   *Fate stands at the threshold.*

In this drama of fate, Akhmatova employs the double theme, not to suggest the hidden side of the human psyche or to tantalize the reader with suggestions of her own unspoken secret, but to explore the interconnectedness of human destinies.

In places, Akhmatova's double theme seems to have the same basic significance that it had in the nineteenth century: the Dostoevskian notion of a soul divided against itself.[27] The figure of "the rival," for whom Blok was the prototype, is a central illustrative instance:

> На стене его твердый профиль.
>   Гавриил или Мефистофель —
>   Твой, красавица, Паладин?
> Демон сам с улыбкой Тамары,
>   Но такие таятся чары
>   В этом страшном дымном лице:
> Плоть, почти что ставшая духом,
>   И античный локон над ухом —

His steely profile is on the wall.
Is your Paladin, O beauty,
Gabriel or Mephistopheles?
The Demon himself with the smile of Tamara,
But such charms lie hidden
In his terrible dusky face;
Flesh which has almost become spirit,
And an antique lock of hair over his ear—

A similar "devil/angel" duality is suggested for the heroine, in the initial symbol of her "black and white fan," in the alternate "portrait" visions of her as Bacchante, Psyche, and "either Columbine or Donna Anna" (this portrait is in shadows), as well as in the author's contradictory epithets for her: "flaxen-haired miracle," "you cheap actress" ("aktërka").

It is important, however, to distinguish between a dual (or ambivalent) authorial vision of these figures and a vision of figures tormented by an internally sensed division. The figures of the poem are not "divided against themselves" in the latter sense; they move without hesitation or apparent conflict toward their fates.

Thus while Akhmatova employs a term spawned in the "delirium" of nineteenth-century Petersburg literary traditions, her usage of it is alien, and in some sense, even antithetical to that earlier meaning. Mr. Golyadkin's confrontation with his double drives him out of his mind and out of his own life; Akhmatova's confrontations with her doubles, of which Sudeykina is only one, culminate in a state of inner wholeness.

For just as the author has "doubled" her manuscript by countless allusions to the works of other writers, so she has multiplied the image of the poet inherent in her own figure with the images of other poets. In "Tails," the author replies to the editor's irritated confusion over the identity of the *Poema's* figures, as follows:

Я ответила: «Там их трое —
Главный был наряжен верстою,

А другой как демон одет, —
Чтоб они столетьям достались,
Их стихи за них постарались...
Третий прожил лишь двадцать лет,
И мне жалко его».

I replied: "There were three of them—
The main one was garbed as a milestone,
But the other was dressed as a demon,—
Their poetry ensured
That they would reach through centuries . . .
The third lived only twenty years,

And I felt sorry for him."

The first point to note is that the author singles out as central to the *Poema* not the love triangle but a trio of poets. Even more unexpected is her singling out of the "striped milestone" as the main figure. This is the figure, in chapter 1's masquerade, who "seems not to be on the list of guests":

Полосатой наряжен верстой, —
Размалеван пестро и грубо —
Ты...
        ровесник Мамврийского дуба,
Вековой собеседник луны.
Не обманут притворные стоны
Ты железные пишешь законы;
Хаммураби, ликурги, солоны
У тебя поучиться должны.
Существо это странного нрава,
Он не ждет, чтоб подагра и слава
Впопыхах усадили его
В юбилейные пышные кресла,
А несет по цветущему вереску
По пустыням свое торжество.

И ни в чем не повинен: ни в этом
    Ни в другом и ни в третьем...
                Поэтам
    Вообще не пристали грехи.
Проплясать пред Ковчегом Завета
    Или сгинуть!..
            Да что там! Про это
    Лучше их рассказали стихи.

Dressed like a striped milestone—
Painted motley and coarsely—
    You . . .
                are as old as the oak of Mamre,
        Ancient interlocutor of the moon.
Feigned moans will not deceive me,
    You write cast-iron laws;
        The Hammurabis, Lycurguses, and Solons
        Should take lessons from you.
A creature of peculiar character,
    He does not wait for gout and glory
        To seat him hastily
            In plush anniversary armchairs,
                But bears his triumph
                    Through blossoming heather and desert.
And is guilty of nothing: not of the first thing,
    Nor the second, nor the third . . .
                    Sins
    In general do not suit poets.
Dance before the Ark of the Covenant
    Or perish! . .
                But why discuss it! Of this
        Their poetry told better.

Everything suggests that Mayakovsky was the prototype of
this complex, contradictory portrait:[28] the costuming reminis-
cent of Mayakovsky's garish Futurist garb, the words "about
that" ("pro eto"), echoing the title of Mayakovsky's famous

poem, and above all, the characterization of the poet as judge and lawmaker. One need only compare these lines of Akhmatova's poem "Mayakovsky v 1913 godu" ("Mayakovsky in 1913," I/241, 1940) to feel certain of knowing who is being referred to in the *Poema*:

В каждом слове бился приговор.

Сумеречной жизнью недоволен,

С нетерпеньем торопил судьбу,

In each word beat a verdict.
Dissatisfied with the twilight life,
He impatiently hurried fate,

The "last year" of the "true nineteenth century," 1913, was not Mayakovsky's twilight but his beginning, the year of the great Futurist tour organized by Burliuk. Perhaps this is why Akhmatova says he is "not on the list of guests." His presence at this ball of ghosts swept away by the new century is thus an ironic commentary on the deceived expectations, not of Mayakovsky alone, but of the Futurists and other poets of that ilk ("of this *their* poetry told better" [italics added]), who hoped for the positive reception of their poetic messages in the new era. Similarly, the reference to his guiltlessness and to the general exemption from sin of the race of poets can only be meant ironically in this work which pounds so insistently upon the themes of sin and retribution.

Why, then, is the "striped milestone" the main figure? The answer would seem to lie in the suggestion of an archetype of the poet, connected to Mayakovsky but not identical with him, which the author treats wholly without irony. Mayakovsky characterized himself as "handsome, twenty-two-year-old," "without a single gray hair in my soul" ("A Cloud in Trousers," 1913), but of the milestone Akhmatova says: "You are as old as the oak of Mamre, ancient interlocutor of the moon." The biblical reference—the plains of Mamre was the setting for the story of Abraham—suggests the stern prophet-poets of the Old Testament ("Dance before the Ark of the Covenant or perish!"), the fiery eternal figure memorialized in Pushkin's "Prophet" ("Prorok"), indifferent to society's honors, who bears his message through the wilderness. Both this pure ideal and its corruption seem to be present in the figure of the "striped milestone."

A further blurring of the outlines of the Mayakovsky figure occurs when it is placed in the light of Akhmatova's poem referring, not to Mayakovsky, but to Blok as "a monument to the beginning of the century" and the "tragic tenor of the epoch." In the *Poema* as well, the Blok figure as the "rival" has been interpreted as representative of "the age." One would expect, then, the term "striped milestone" to refer to Blok, and indeed, at least one critic has assumed that it does.[29]

Blok, however, is the figure to whom Akhmatova refers in "Tails" as "a demon." According to the above-quoted portrait of him, he is at least half-demon ("Gabriel or Mephistopheles? The Demon himself with the smile of Tamara") and as such an embodiment of the "lame and elegant" "King of Darkness" whose spirit rules the "hellish harlequinade" of 1913. The key to Blok's demonic nature is suggested in the lines:

> Все таинственно в пришлеце.
> Это он в переполненном зале
>   Слал ту черную розу в бокале,
>   Или все это было сном?..

> *Everything about this visitor is mystery.*
> *Was it he in that overcrowded hall*
>   *Who sent the black rose in the wine glass,*
>   *Or was all that a dream? . .*

In the poem "V restorane" ("In the Restaurant," 1910) from which the black rose image is taken, Blok himself asks the same question concerning the reality of that which he describes:

Никогда не забуду (он был, или не был,
Этот вечер):

I shall never forget (did it happen, or not happen,
That evening):

The line between "true" vision and deceptive illusion constantly vacillates in Blok's poetry, an "instability" which forms a central axis of his poetic world. Perhaps the "demon half" of Blok expresses his contradictory nature as idealist, creator of divine visions, and cynic, who recognizes the actual bleakness of reality, the one of whom Akhmatova wrote: "He's right: again, drugstore, street lamp." He would thus correspond to the demon of Gogol's "Nevsky Prospect" (a Petersburg street which plays a major role in Blok's own poetry), who "himself lights all the street lamps to show everything in anything but its true colors."

But if Blok, as the creator of illusions he himself discredits, is "villain," he is also victim of a reality he understood better than anyone:

С мертвым сердцем и мертвым взором,
Он ли встретился с командором,
В тот пробравшись проклятый дом!

With lifeless heart and lifeless gaze,
Was it he who met the commendatore,
Having penetrated into that cursed house?

These lines, which place Blok within the scenario of his own poem, "The Steps of the Commendatore," parallel the description of Blok by one of his contemporaries: "For us Blok became a tragic actor who played himself. . . . His youthful figure had been fused with his poetry in the same way in which the make-up of a tragic actor is inseparable from his monologue. Each time Blok appeared before us, we felt a

shiver down our spines. So much did he resemble himself."[30]
Blok then becomes the poet who is doomed by his own con-
summate understanding of his age.

The final poet figure, the one who "died at twenty" be-
gins, but by no means ends, with the prototype of Vsevolod
Knyazev, whose single volume of poetry, apparently not des-
tined to "reach through centuries," was published post-
humously, the year after his death. Hovering about the figure
and actions of Knyazev is his spiritual double, Osip Man-
delstam, whose date of death prefaces the first dedication
and whose words "I am ready to die" are placed on Knyazev's
lips at the moment of his suicide. In spite of her "grievance"
at Akhmatova's "misappropriation" of Mandelstam's words
and the date of his death "for the sake of a literary game,"
Nadezhda Mandelstam grudgingly admits that "if the *Poem
Without a Hero* is supposed to be about two people, one
of whom took his own life before the beginning of our new
era, while the other accepted his lot unflinchingly, then the
meaning of the work takes on a somewhat wider sense."[31]
N. Mandelstam's interpretation assumes that the Knyazev-
Mandelstam juxtaposition is primarily a contrasting of moral
alternatives: Knyazev's representing the moral "license"
("proizvolie") of his suicide-prone generation, about which
she herself writes so penetratingly in her memoirs; and Man-
delstam's, representing the highest level of personal and
artistic responsibility. But while it is true that the author
"scolds" the cornet for choosing this early death, when so
many others awaited him, her attitude toward the event is not
limited to one of moral disapproval. The significance of
the suicide is underscored by its repetition, in chapters 1
and 4, accompanied, each time, by the cornet's almost identi-
cal words:

«*Прощай! Пора!*
Я оставлю тебя живою,
Но ты будешъ м о е й вдовою,
Ты — Голубка, солнце, сестра!»

> "Farewell! It's time!
> *I am leaving you alive,*
> *But you will be* my *widow,*
> *You are my Dove, my sun, my sister!"*
> > [Chapter 1]

> «Ты, Голубка, солнце, сестра!
> Я оставлю тебя живою,
> > Но ты будешь м о е й вдовою,
> > А теперь...
> > > Прощаться пора!»

> "You, my Dove, my sun, my sister!
> *I will leave you alive,*
> > *But you will be* my *widow,*
> > *And now . . .*
> > > *It's time to say goodbye!"*
> > > > [Chapter 4]

The names with which the cornet addresses his beloved—
Dove, sun, sister ("Golubka," "solntse," "sestra") are impor-
tant Mandelstammian words, appearing, in his poetry, in a
positive context, often in association with the idea of poetry: [32]

Сестры — тяжесть и нежность — одинаковы ваши приметы.

Sisters—heaviness and tenderness, your signs are identical.

Ничего, голубка Эвридика,
Что у нас студеная зима.

Never mind, dove, Euridice,
That our winter is frozen.

В Петербурге мы сойдемся снова,
Словно солнце мы похоронили в нем,

In Petersburg we will meet again,
As if we had buried the sun there,

Возьми на радость из моих ладоней
Немного солнца и немного меда,

Take for joy from my palms
A little sun and a little honey,

When Akhmatova says

И драгунский корнет со стихами
И с бессмысленной смертью в груди

And a dragoon cornet with poetry
And senseless death in his heart

she uses the word "bessmyslennaia"—which, for Mandel-
stam signified the divine "foolishness," that is, the aration-
ality of the poetic word. Thus in Mandelstam's "We will meet
again in Petersburg":

В Петербурге мы сойдемся снова,
Словно солнце мы похоронили в нем,
И блаженное, бессмысленное слово
В первый раз произнесем.

In Petersburg we will meet again,
As if we had buried the sun there.
And the blessed, senseless word
We will speak for the first time.

And again, in the same poem:

За блаженное бессмысленное слово
Я в ночи советской помолюсь.

> *For the blessed, senseless word*
> *I will pray in the Soviet night.*

All this strongly suggests that on a symbolic level, the cornet's "foolish" death is a death in honor of an ideal, the ideal of art and beauty which Sudeykina represents to him. In this sense, Mandelstam's death, too, was a form of "suicide"; he chose death by choosing to remain himself, the deepest essence of which was a dedication to the ideal of poetry. If the cornet's rival in the *Poema* is, symbolically, the age, so was Mandelstam's, albeit a later one and part of the new Soviet era. Knyazev died before the upheaval of the First World War and all that was to follow; Mandelstam's death in 1938 preceded the holocaust of the Second World War, which would bring yet another cycle of death and resurrection to the city on the Neva. Although one struck only a few, quickly fading notes and the other sounded an enduring chord, both were part of the ongoing, fateful music of Petersburg-Leningrad.

A City between Two Worlds

Parallel to the tenuous, continually shifting, and dissolving nature of the *Poema's* masks, shades, doubles, mirror-images, and living portraits is the vacillating reality of the city itself. Just as the House on the Fontanka provides a "threshold" for the meeting of the author and the ghosts of 1913, so the *Poema's* larger spatial context, the city of Peter-Petersburg-Leningrad is the malleable, continually transforming medium—

Значит, мягче воска гранит...

So granite is softer than wax . . .

—exempt from the usual restrictions of time and space, through which Akhmatova expresses her sense of human history:

И его поведано словом,
   Как вы были в пространстве новом,
      Как вне времени были вы —
И в каких хрусталях полярных,
   И в каких сияньях янтарных
      Там, у устья Леты — Невы.
Ты сбежала сюда с портрета,
   И пустая рама до света
      На стене тебя будет ждать.

And has it been told in his words,
   How you were in a new space,
      How you were outside time—
And in what polar crystals,
   And in what amber gleamings
      There at the mouth of the Lethe-Neva.
You fled here from your portrait,
   And the empty frame on the wall
      Will wait for you till dawn.

In commenting on this central passage, Dolgopolov makes this key observation: "Petersburg, continuing to remain the city of 'Nevsky Prospect,' *The Bronze Horseman,* and *Crime and Punishment,* takes on additional features which place this terrible, fantastic, half-real, 'abstract' city on the boundary of being, transform it into some kind of bewitched place, situated somewhere between this world and the next."[33] He locates the source of Akhmatova's vision in Bely's novel, in whose first chapter the author speaks of the river's "Lethean waters" and notes that Akhmatova has a similar vision of the city as a place where people turn to shadows and vice versa.

In Akhmatova's previous Petersburg poetry, the implied identification of Lethe and the Neva occurs in the early love poem "Flight." Akhmatova uses the phrase explicitly for the first time in her 1940 poem to Lozinsky, "Nadpis' na knige" ("Inscription in a Book," I/229):

Почти от залетейской тени
В тот час, как рушатся миры,
Примите этот дар весенний
В ответ на лучшие дары,
Чтоб та, над временами года,
Несокрушима и верна,
Души высокая свобода,
Что дружбою наречена, —
Мне улыбнулась так же кротко,
Как тридцать лет тому назад...
И сада Летнего решетка,
И оснеженный Ленинград
Возникли, словно в книге этой
Из мглы магических зеркал,
И над задумчивою Летой
Тростник оживший зазвучал.

From a shade almost beyond Lethe
At this hour, when worlds are being destroyed,
Accept this spring gift
In answer to better gifts,
So that above the seasons of the year,
Indestructible and faithful,
The high freedom of the soul,
Betrothed to us by friendship,
Will smile at me humbly,
As it did thirty years ago . . .
And the ironwork of the Summer Garden
And snow-covered Leningrad will rise up,
Just as in this book
From the mists of magical mirrors,
And above thoughtful Lethe
The revived reed will sound.[34]

Speaking of this poem, and the many personal losses
Akhmatova had borne by this time, Haight remarks, "Cer-

tainly at times she must have felt as if she herself were already dead."[35] But Akhmatova here calls herself "a shade *almost* beyond Lethe" (italics added); both she and her city lay hidden in "the mists of magical mirrors." The reappearance of the lost city occurs in a realm outside of time ("Above the seasons of the year") and is simultaneous with the rebirth of poetry ("the revived reed will sound"). In this poem, written a few months before Akhmatova started work on the *Poema*, the Lethe-Neva is an elegiac theme, imbued with the ideal of ennobling friendship, in which both poetry and the beloved past endure.

But in other poems of the early 1940s "ghostly Leningrad" is a tormented theme, an image of the city's wartime martyrdom; in the postwar poems, Akhmatova is herself not the shade but a mourner, surrounded by a growing community of shades, endlessly observing the "unforgettable, accursed dates" of loss, of her Leningrad calendar. Later, in the 1950s the shades of the past are joined by other emanations of a nonmaterial world: the footsteps of he who has not come, the blessed memory of meetings which have not occurred.

In the *Poem without a Hero*, Akhmatova's shadow city moves closer to the city of Bely's *Petersburg*, where the city's masks, doubles, the circular transformation of matter into shadow and back again, express the instability and chaotic nature of a world on the verge of destruction.

> . . . oh, Russian people, oh, Russian people, don't let the crowd of shadows in from the islands! Black and damp bridges are already thrown across the waters of Lethe. If only they could be dismantled . . .
> Too late . . .
> And the shadows thronged across the bridge. And the dark shadow of the stranger.[36]

As in Bely, the notion of approaching doom permeates Akhmatova's spectral city, and as in the earlier novel, the general catastrophe, developed as both social revolution and cosmic apocalypse, is indissolubly bound to a disastrous love triangle.

Akhmatova develops the "personal apocalypse" both through the Knyazev-Sudeykina-Blok triangle and through the poem's numerous allusions to the Don Juan of Pushkin, Blok, Molière, Byron, Mozart. The sense of inescapable tragedy is reinforced by its multiple reflections in the text: the scene of the suicide is presented twice, in chapters 1 and 4 of part 1. The image of Don Juan meeting his retribution at the hands of the Commendatore is reflected from many different angles, so that the cornet's death (at his own hands, but spurred by his "rival"—the invincible age) appears as but one instance of a recurring drama.

But the *Poema*'s larger, encompassing image of retribution is the city itself, alternately appearing as Pursued and Pursuer, Don Juan and the Commendatore. In chapters 1 and 2, Akhmatova establishes a consistent contrast between the "inner space" of the masquerade and the heroine's bedroom, where images of the reawakened past stand whole, and the "external space" of a winter city, both historical and legendary, which threatens to engulf them. The first of these images is the Neva, since Pushkin the foremost Petersburg image of impending chaos:

> За окошком Нева дымится,
>   Ночь бездонна и длится, длится —
>   Петербургская чертовня...

> *Beyond the window smokes the Neva,*
>   *Unfathomable is the night—*
>   *And on and on goes the Petersburg diaboliad . . .*

In chapter 2, the space outside the heroine's bedroom window is evoked as "Peter":

А вокруг старый город Питер, —
Что народу бока повытер,
(Как тогда народ говорил).

And all around is old "Peter" city,—
Which wore out people's hides,
(As the people said at the time).

Through the old proverb, which arose in Peter's time, when the city was being built, Akhmatova places the remembered prerevolutionary times within the historical context of the city's "original sin," its construction at the cost of countless human lives; both the city's cruelty and its "transgression" against the people, which must some day be paid for, are evoked.

At this point in the *Poema*, the alternation between inner and outer space becomes one of "artistic space"—the triumphant portraits of Pavlova and Chalyapin—and the outdoor "stage setting" for the fifth act of the city's tragedy:

До смешного близка развязка:
Из-за ширм Петрушкина маска,
Вкруг костров кучерская пляска,
Над дворцом черно-желтый стяг...
Все уже на местах, кто надо;
Пятым актом из Летнего сада
Пахнет... Призрак цусимского ада
Тут же. — Пьяный поет моряк.
Как парадно звенят полозья,
И волочится полость козья...
Мимо, тени!

The denouement is ridiculously close;
From behind the screen Petrushka's mask,
A coachman's dance around the bonfires,
Over the palace a blackish-yellow standard.

> *All who are necessary are in their places;*
> *The Summer Garden smells of*
> *Act Five . . . The phantom of the hell of Tsushima*
> *Is here too.—A drunken sailor sings.*
> *How gaily the sled-runners zing*
> *And the goat-fur lap robe drags along . . .*
> *Pass by, shades! . . .*

Reminiscences of Mandelstam are present in the image of the "blackish-yellow standard," which echoes a line from Mandelstam's 1915 poem of the old capital's disintegration— "Palace Square":

> Только там, где твердь светла,
> Черно-желтый лоскут злится,
> Словно в воздухе струится
> Желчь двуглавого орла.

> *Only there, where the firmament is bright,*
> *A blackish-yellow rag is angry,*
> *As if the bile of the two-headed eagle*
> *Were streaming in the air.*

But above all, Mandelstam is evoked through the juxtaposition of what Segal[37] has called "the internal, warm and illuminated space of the theatre and external, frosty, and 'black' space" of a winter world, in which the image of coachmen and bonfires play a prominent role (see "Chut' mertsaet prizrachnaia stsena," "The ghostly stage barely glimmers").

It is characteristic of Akhmatova's apocalyptic cityscapes, however, that the external space, contrasted with the world of art, is itself "framed" within a "stage setting." Viewed against the background of the long and brilliant tradition of Petersburg's apocalyptic "poems," Akhmatova's is distinguished by its great remove in time from the events described. Consequently, her visions of Petersburg on the edge of the abyss have a quality less of fearful expectation than of poetic summary. In chapter 3's full-scale portrait of the Petersburg of 1913, toward which the previous city images have been building, she snatches chords from her own Petersburg music, from Mandelstam's and Lozinsky's; she merges the curse of Peter's first wife, Tsaritsa Avdotya, abandoned for a German bride and forced into a nunnery: "May this place be barren!" with the "Dostoevskian and possessed" city of the great nineteenth-century novelist; she speaks in the voice of Blok's cosmic wind (*The Twelve*) and listens to the prophetic "rumble" ("gul") of Bely's *Petersburg* and Blok's *The Twelve*. But her apocalyptic tableaux have the roundedness, authority, and clarity which can only be conveyed long after the event, by one who well knows the nature of the "rough beast slouching toward Jerusalem":

> Были Святки кострами согреты,
> И валились с мостов кареты,
> И весь траурный город плыл
> По неведомому назначенью
> По Неве иль против теченья, —
> Только прочь от своих могил.
> На Галерной чернела арка,
> В Летнем тонко пела флюгарка,
> И серебряный месяц ярко
> Над серебряным веком стыл.
> Оттого, что по всем дорогам,
> Оттого, что ко всем порогам
> Приближалась медленно тень —
> Ветер рвал со стены афиши,
> Дым плясал вприсядку на крыше
> И кладбищем пахла сирень.
> И царицей Авдотьей заклятый,
> Достоевский и бесноватый
> Город в свой уходил туман,
> И выглядывал вновь из мрака
> Старый питерщик и гуляка.
> Как пред казнью бил барабан...

И всегда в духоте морозной,
Предвоенной, блудной и грозной,
Непонятный таился гул...
Но тогда он был слышен глухо,
Он почти не касался слуха
И в сугробах невских тонул.
Словно в зеркале страшной ночи
И беснуется и не хочет
Узнавать себя человек, —
А по набережной легендарной
Приближался не календарный —
Настоящий Двадцатый Век.

Christmas was warmed by bonfires,
And carriages fell off the bridges,
And the whole funereal city swam
Toward some enigmatic goal
Along the Neva's current or against it—
Anything to head away from its graves.
On Gallery Street stood the black archway,
A weathervane sang thinly in the Summer Garden.
And a moon of vivid silver.
Froze over the Silver Age.
Because on every road,
Because to every threshold
A shade was slowly drawing near—
The wind was tearing posters from the walls,
Smoke whirled in cossack dances on the roof
And the lilac smelled of the cemetery.
And cursed by Tsaritsa Avdotya,
Dostoevskian and possessed
The City disappeared into its mist.
And again it peered out of the darkness
Old Petersburger and drunkard.
A drum rolled as before an execution . . .
And always in the atmosphere of frozen suffocation,

> *In the pre-war, prodigal, menacing air,*
>   *An incomprehensible rumble lurked . . .*
> *But then it was hollowly audible,*
>   *It scarcely touched one's ears at all*
>   *And drowned in Nevsky's snowdrifts.*
> *As if in the mirror of a terrible night*
>   *Man rages and does not wish*
>   *To recognize himself—*
> *While along the legendary quay*
>   *Approached not the calendar—*
>   *But the True Twentieth Century.*

"And My City Stands Mended"

What path does the author take from the accursed city of the True Twentieth Century in order to arrive at the beloved, "mended" city of the "Epilogue"? The question is not one of form—logical transitions are alien to the *Poema's* structure—but of an underlying philosophy of history.

In her epigraphs to this section, Akhmatova deliberately juxtaposes the accursed and the beloved cities:

> *Люблю мебя, Петра творенье!*
>   *Медный всадник*

> *I love thee, creation of Peter!*
>   *The Bronze Horseman*

> *Быть пусту месту сему...*

> *May this place be barren . . .*

> *Да пустыни немых тлощадей,*
> *Где казнили людей до рассвета*
>   *Анненский*

> *And the deserts of mute city squares,*
> *Where people were executed before dawn*
>   Annensky

Does she intend for them to stand before the reader, in the *Poema* as a whole, as well, as two antithetical visions; or is there another, integrative relationship between them?

Haight suggests a solution based on the well-known sense of relief and national unity experienced by Russians at the outbreak of a war which, however terrible, freed them from the Terror of the 1930s:

> In "Epilogue" it is Leningrad-Petersburg, the city once cursed by Eudoxia, wife of Peter the Great, the city of Dostoevsky, that becomes the hero of the poem. In its crucifixion at the time of the blockade Akhmatova found the symbol for all that she had meant by the "True Twentieth Century." Just as her role as a poet had ceased to be something of solely individual significance, so individual suffering had become one with the suffering of the city which now reached its apex as bombed from above; its citizens slowly died of cold and starvation. The horrors of the war were, however, faced collectively, not singly as during the Terror.[38]

Certainly, there is much to be said for this argument; the full-scale "rehabilitation" of Leningrad in Akhmatova's war poems, from the "prison city" she had perceived in the 1930s, is evidence of the resurgence of the sense of national unity Haight describes.

The city of the "Epilogue" is the heroic, martyred city of the siege; but it is more than that. Akhmatova brings it into relationship with all that has been described in the first part of the *Poema*, with the furthest reaches of her personal past and with a suprapersonal future.

Her conception in the "Epilogue" is illuminated by the materials she accumulated, during the late 1950s, under the heading "Pages from a Diary," ("Listki iz dnevnika"),[39] which were intended for a projected autobiographical book. The sketch of the table of contents alone indicates the central role she allotted in her personal history to the role of the city:

I. (Pro domo mea)
1. Biography
2. Fates
3. The City
4. About the lyric
5. The Fate of Acmeism[40]

The summaries and excerpts from Akhmatova's unfinished sketches, offered by Mandrykina in her article describing the contents of the "Unfinished Book," indicate Akhmatova's essentially factual approach in attempting to record the appearance and customs of the city in its successive incarnations. One note, pointing to the author's overall intentions, is of particular interest with respect to the *Poema*:

> After Petersburg as I found it (at that time I was only an observer, in the full sense of the word), I will say a few words about the Petersburg of the 'teens, about wartime Petersburg, about revolutionary Petrograd. About the unforgettable (but for some reason wholly forgotten) year of 1919 and finally, about post-blockade Leningrad. So many layers! These themes are haphazardly touched upon in my "Poem Without a Hero," I described post-blockade Leningrad in detail when I returned from Tashkent (from the Evacuation).[41]

Mandrykina notes:

> A second sketch about Petersburg is "Outline." Finding in the image of the city features linking the Petersburg of the beginning of the 19th century and Petersburg of the teens of the 20th century with Leningrad of the

1920s and 1940s, the author, like a true resident of the city on the Neva, says: "All this is my Leningrad." [42]

What these excerpts point to is a vision of the city as a many-layered temporal structure, the levels of which, though vividly distinct from one another, are yet bound to one another through an internal essence existing outside of the compartmentalization of historic periods. In the *Poema*, the juxtaposition of the years 1913, just before the advent of World War I and the True Twentieth Century, and 1942, the time of the blockade, is a medium for the discovery of the city's atemporal essence.

The introductory prose segment describing the scene is a key to what follows:

> Белая ночь 24 июня 1942 г. Город в развалинах. От Гавани до Смольного видно все как на ладони. Кое-где догорают застарелые пожары. В Шереметевском саду цветут липы и поет соловей. Одно окно третьего этажа (перед которым увечный клен) выбито, и за ним зияет черная пустота. В стороне Кронштадта ухают тяжелые орудия. Но в общем тихо. Голос автора, находящегося за семь тысяч километров, произносит:

> The white night of June 24, 1942. The city is in ruins. From the Harbor to the Smolny everything is flattened and visible. Here and there old fires are burning themselves out. Lindens are blooming and a nightingale is singing in the Sheremetev Gardens. One third-floor window (in front of which there is an injured maple) is knocked out, and beyond it yawns black emptiness. From the direction of Kronstadt, heavy guns are audible. But in general, it is quiet. From seven thousand kilometers away, the author's voice speaks.

In the midst of the ruined city, nature survives. Lindens bloom, just as they did in the Summer Garden, in Akhmatova's 1914 poem "That voice, arguing with the great silence," which evoked the "armed camp" city of the First World War. Here they represent renewal, not only of nature, but of the city itself. Although the "Epilogue" presents a landscape of doom parallel to that of 1913, there is no trace of apocalyptic anxiety in the author's voice. If the cataclysm of 1913 is presented as a single, irreversible event, 1942 appears as part of a cyclical process of the city's deaths and resurrections. An indication of this cyclicity appears in the prose description at the beginning of "Fourth and Last Chapter":

> Угол Марсова поля. Дом, построенный в начале XIX века братьями Адамини. В него будет прямое попадание авиабомбы в 1942 году. Горит высокий костер. Слышны удары колокольного звона от Спаса-на-Крови. На поле за метелью призрак дворцового бала.

> A corner of Mars Field. The building built at the beginning of the XIXth century by the brothers Adamini. In 1942 it will suffer a direct hit from a bomb. A huge bonfire is burning. The tolling bell of Our Savior on the Blood Cathedral is heard. On the field, through the snowstorm, the phantom of a palace ball.

By situating the cornet's death in a place bound up with the tragedies of the past—the vicinity of Mars Field, which, as I previously noted, Akhmatova associated with the assassinations of Paul and Alexander—and the future holocaust, Akhmatova places the event within a long procession of Petersburg-Leningrad catastrophes.

In the "Epilogue," this theme of the "city of recurring disasters" repeats, but with the emphasis changed to stress the notions of recovery and survival, now closely bound up with the figure of the author herself. Like the city, the author has passed through many cycles of "death and resurrection." In the (later omitted) lines to Garshin, she tells him

Ты не первый и не последний
    Темный слушатель светлых бредней,

You are not the first and not the last
    Dark listener of bright nonsense,

She appears as one who has survived, and will continue to survive, both Love and History. Her final "double," significantly, is one who has not survived. The far-off lands, "outside the city," become the landscape of her alternate fate: death in a camp of the True Twentieth Century.

А за проволокой колючей,
В самом сердце тайги дремучей —
Я не знаю, который год —
Ставший горстью лагерной пыли,
Ставший сказкой из страшной были,
Мой двойник на допрос идет.
А потом он идет с допроса,
Двум посланцам Девки безносой
Суждено охранять его.

But behind the barbed wire,
In the very heart of the dense taiga—
I don't know how many years it's been—
Turned into a handful of prison-camp dust,
Turned into a fairytale from a true and terrifying tale,
My double goes to the interrogation.
Then he returns from the interrogation,
Two emissaries of the Noseless Wench
Are fated to guard him.

In the lines immediately following, she speaks of her actual fate, which was "to walk for exactly ten years under the threat of a Nagan pistol," once more evoking the "prison city" of the 1930s. But the central fact about the city, however threatening it may have been, is that it has *not* become her grave.

А не ставший моей могилой,
  Ты, гранитный, кромешный, милый,
    Побледнел, помертвел, затих.

And without becoming my grave,
  You, granite, hellish, beloved,
    You grew pale, moribund, and quiet.

As in the 1936 poem "Dante," where she spoke of "his longed-for Florence, treacherous, base, long-awaited," Akhmatova resurrects the archetype of the "native and accursed, desired and inaccessible city of the banished poet,"[43] while simultaneously denying the reality of that banishment. Writing on top of her own 1913 "Verses about Petersburg," she declares:

Разлучение наше мнимо:
  Я с тобою неразлучима,
    Тень моя на стенах твоих,
Отраженье мое в каналах,
  Звук шагов в Эрмитажных залах,
    Где со мною мой друг бродил,
И на старом Волковом Поле,
  Где могу я рыдать на воле
    Над безмолвьем братских могил.

Our separation is transient:
  I am inseparable from you,
    My shadow is on your walls,
My reflection is in your canals,
    The sound of my footsteps in the Hermitage halls,
      Where my friend wandered with me,
And on old Volkov Field,
    Where I can sob at will
      Over the noiselessness of fraternal graves.

If, in the earlier poem, participation in the eternal life of the city assured the immortality of the love relationship ("And

under the archway on Gallery Street our shades will always
be"), here the priority of connections has been reordered:
what is foremost is the inseparability of the city and the poet,
whose fate, both loves and losses, has been lived out within
its precincts. It is this affirmation which leads to her assertion:

Все, что сказано в Первой части
   О любви, измене и страсти,
      Сбросил с крыльев свободный стих,
И стоит мой город зашитый...

All that was said in Part One
   About love, betrayal and passion,
      Free verse cast from its wings,
And my city stands mended . . .[44]

It is in these lines that the author deliberately reconciles the
"accursed" and "beloved" cities of the *Poema*. They imply that
the process of poetic creation has itself been the medium
for a purging—both of the author's soul and of the sins of
the city.[45]

Having passed through this artistic crucible, the events
of 1913 are now seen as the eternal human drama of "love,
betrayal and passion"; their wholly damning, demonic quality
has been stripped from them. The Judgment Day has come,
and gone. Petersburg has vanished and has reappeared.
Reflected in the mirrors of their distant but kindred ca-
tastrophes, the years 1913 and 1942 offer one another the re-
assurance of a difficult survival.

Akhmatova expresses her final affirmation of the city
with the unusual phrase: My city stands "mended." ("Stoit
moi gorod zashityi"), which, Zhirmunsky explains,[46] refers to
the boarding up of Leningrad's windows during the time of
the bombardment. On the physical level, then, "mended"
suggests not wholeness but disfiguration. But the boarded
windows are a sign of the city's defensive posture. Through
this word play Akhmatova implies that the city's wholeness is

precisely in its continual struggle to survive the devastations of successive eras. It is this ongoing city which lends a lyrical, almost tranquil beauty to the martyred Leningrad of 1942:

> Тяжелы надгробные плиты
>> На бессонных очах твоих.
> Мне казалось, за мной ты гнался,
>> Ты, что там погибать остался
>>> В блеске шпилей, в отблеске вод.
> Не дождался желанных вестниц...
>> Над тобой — лишь твоих прелестниц,
>>> Белых ноченек хоровод.

> *Heavy are the gravestones*
>> *On your sleepless eyes.*
> *It seemed to me that you were chasing me,*
>> *You who stayed there to perish*
>>> *In the gleam of spires and reflection of waters.*
> *Your desired lovely heralds didn't come . . .*
>> *Only the chorus of your charmers,*
>>> *The white nights pass over you.*

At a time when "the happy words 'at home' are not known to anyone," the city under perpetual siege is Home; not in a narrow, domestic or even nationalistic sense but, in the sense of Mandelstam's phrase, "man's place in the universe."

Notes

1. With minor alterations, all English quotations from the *Poema* represent the translation of Carl R. Proffer and Assya Humesky (Ann Arbor: Ardis, 1973). The textual problems of the *Poema*, written and rewritten over the span of a quarter century, are well known to Akhmatova specialists and are considered "perhaps ultimately insoluble" by at least one (Proffer, "*A Poem without a Hero*: Notes and Commentary," in *A Poem without a Hero*, trans. Proffer and

Humesky, p. 39). Following Proffer's example, I will be using the text Amanda Haight said Akhmatova herself checked while visiting Oxford and pronounced final. This text corresponds almost entirely to that printed in Struve. I will, however, also make reference to variations presented by V. Zhirmunsky in his edition of Akhmatova's work. Zhirmunsky had access to the Akhmatova archives in Leningrad, but this advantage was offset by the realities of Soviet censorship, hence the omission of such "politically" laden lines as those from the "Epilogue" dealing with the Terror (beginning with "But behind the barbed wire . . ."). (See Berlin, *Personal Impressions*, for an account of Zhirmunsky's distress at having to bow to political considerations in his preparation of the text, p. 199.)

2. Berlin, *Personal Impressions*, p. 194.

3. Haight, *Akhmatova*, p. 156.

4. Nadezhda Mandelstam, *Hope Abandoned* (New York: Atheneum, 1974), p. 435.

5. O. Mandelstam, *Collected Works*, ed. Struve and Filippov, 2:76.

6. See N. Mandelstam's descriptions of how she persuaded Akhmatova of the accuracy of this date, *Hope Abandoned*, pp. 433–34.

7. See Chukovskaya, *Zapiski*, 2:179, where she quotes Akhmatova as saying, "'Osip had thick eyelashes, to the middle of his cheeks . . .' ('And Antinous' dark lashes,' I instantly remembered. Then to whom are these lines dedicated—to Mandelstam or to Knyazev?)" Chukovskaya indicates that she will deal with this question in her forthcoming book, *House of the Poet*.

8. N. Mandelstam, *Hope Abandoned*, p. 436.

9. Vsevolod Knyazev's *Poems* was published posthumously in 1914 in St. Petersburg.

10. Because of the large amount of sometimes overlapping scholarship on Akhmatova's literary allusions, it is not always possible to identify these discoveries with specific scholars. The basic research on Blok's role was done by Zhirmunsky ("Akhmatova i Blok," pp. 57–82). An analysis of Blok's and Dostoevsky's roles as the two poles of the poem is contained in L. K. Dolgopolov, "Po zakonam pritiazheniia" ("By the Laws of Attraction"), *Russkaia literatura*, no. 4 (1979), pp. 38–58. The *Poema*'s relationship to Kuzmin's 'Forel' razbivait lëd" ("Trout Breaks the Ice") is treated by R. Timenchik, *Materialy XXII nauchnoi studencheskoi konferentsii* (*Materials of the Twenty-Second Academic Student Conference*) (Tartu, 1967), pp. 121–23.

Foreign authors who figure in the poem include Shelley, Byron, T. S. Eliot, Oscar Wilde, Dumas, Molière, and Merimée.

11. Berlin, *Personal Impressions*, p. 198.

12. N. Mandelstam, *Hope Abandoned*, p. 429.

13. See O. Ronen, "Leksicheskii povtor, podtekst i smysl' v poetike Osipa Mandelstama" ("Lexical Repetition, Subtext, and Meaning in the Poetics of Osip Mandelstam"), *Slavic Poetics: Essays in Honor of Kiril Taranovsky* (The Hague: Mouton, 1973), p. 371.

14. The first critic to note this aspect of Mandelstam's work was V. M. Zhirmunsky, in "Preodelevshie Simvolizma" ("Those Who Overcame Symbolism"), *Russkaia mysl'* (*Russian Thought*), no. 12 (1916), pp. 41–49. The original phrase "die Poesie der Poesie" belongs to Schiller.

15. O. Mandelstam, *Collected Works*, ed. Struve and Filippov, 2:266.

16. See my introduction for a discussion of the "fantastic city."

17. See Zhirmunsky's note to the phrase "that midnight Hoffmaniana" which appears in chapter 1 of the *Poema*: "In her notes to the poema . . . , Akhmatova speaks of its link to the Petersburg Hoffmaniana (implying Gogol's Petersburg tales, Dostoevsky's 'The Double' and Andrey Bely's *Petersburg*." *Akhmatova: Stikhotvoreniia i poemy*, p. 514.

18. Verheul, *Theme of Time*, p. 185.

19. Ibid., p. 43.

20. Mandrykina, " 'Nenapisannaia kniga,' p. 63.

21. This idea is supported by Akhmatova's remark to Chukovskaya (*Zapiski*, 2:446): "1913 is spoken of through Hoffmaniana, but 1941 with full realistic clarity."

22. Dolgopolov, "Po zakonam," sees the masquerade as a European tradition: "It is hardly accidental that the New Year's Ball in the House on the Fontanka is reminiscent of an imagined carnival procession on the square of a European capital" (p. 48). His argument is that Akhmatova wishes to present a Petersburg which is both Europe and non-Europe. While it is true that the masquerade tradition originated in Europe, its adaptation within Russian life and literature is well enough established to make the masquerade a Russian (Petersburg) tradition as well.

23. The masquerade in F. Sologub's *Melkii bes* (*The Petty Demon*) is another Russian masquerade of "evil spirits," with which Akhmatova was certainly familiar. The "hellish harlequinade" which

Sologub presents is, however, a part more of the provincial hell than of the Petersburg one.

The *Poema* specifically alludes to the Walpurgisnacht of Goethe's *Faust* as another model.

24. Zhirmunsky says of the necklace: "Thus was Akhmatova depicted in a portrait" (*Akhmatova: Stikhotvoreniia i poemy*, p. 514), but he does not identify the painting in question. There are several photographs of Akhmatova wearing a necklace of black beads.

25. Nadezhda Mandelstam has written of Akhmatova's "preoccupation with doubles" as

> something rooted in her psychology, a result of her attitude to people—in whom, as in mirrors, she always sought her own reflection. She looked at people as one might look into a mirror, hoping to find her own likeness and seeing her "double" in everybody. She described Olga Sudeikina as "one of my doubles" and Marina Tsvetaeva as a "mocking double, out of sight"; and she once dedicated a book to me with the words: "To my second self." . . . In fairness to Akhmatova, however, I must say that, apart from the element of self-centeredness, it was due as well to another quality which she displayed in high degree: a capacity to become so highly involved in others that she had the need to tie them to herself as closely as possible, to merge herself in them. This was particularly so in the case of those many women on whom she conferred the status of "beauties." [*Hope Abandoned*, p. 437]

26. Jeanne Van der Eng-Liedmeier in *Tale without a Hero* and *Twenty-Two Poems by Anna Akhmatova* (The Hague: Mouton, 1973), p. 94. She quotes Verheul's observation that Akhmatova may have "considered herself in a sense responsible" for the death of her close friend, N. A. Nedobrovo, who died in 1919, p. 92 (see Verheul, *Theme of Time*, pp. 86, 91). While the experience is interesting from a biographical point of view, the attempt to weight it with responsibility for the guilt of the fictional author of the *Poema* seems to me only to limit the work's scope and relevance.

27. See Dolgopolov, "Po zakonam," p. 45. Dolgopolov sees in the Blok figure the Dostoevskian model of the divided hero.

28. Ibid., p. 40. Dolgopolov interprets this figure as Blok but, in a footnote, details the evidence for the "second possibility" that the fig-

ure is Mayakovsky. See Chukovskaya, *Zapiski*, 2:411: "Tsvetaeva, speaking about Mayakovsky, uses the expression 'he pokes his finger, like a striped milepost, into things.' Isn't this the source of the *Poema's*—'garbed like a striped milepost'? (Akhmatova often borrows what she likes from others, sometimes consciously, sometimes forgetting where it's from.)"

29. See n. 28.

30. Boris Eikhenbaum, "Sud'ba Bloka" ("Blok's Fate"), *Skvoz' literaturu* (*Through Literature*) (Leningrad, 1924), quoted in Victor Erlich, *The Double Image* (Baltimore: Johns Hopkins University Press, 1964), p. 100.

31. N. Mandelstam, *Hope Abandoned*, p. 435.

32. Of these three words, "solntse" appears with the greatest frequency. See Demetrius J. Koubourlis, *A Concordance to the Poems of Osip Mandelstam* (Ithaca and London: Cornell University Press, 1974), pp. 512–13. The word "golub'" and related forms are frequent in Mandelstam. Although the term "golubka" as a form of address to a woman occurs only once, its context within the Petersburg theater poem "Chut' mertsaet prizrachnaia stsena" ("The ghostly stage barely glimmers") strongly associates it with Akhmatova's theme of the lost prerevolutionary artistic world.

33. Dolgopolov, "Po zakonam," p. 47.

34. Cf. Tyutchev's poem "Opiat' stoiu ia nad Nevoi" ("Again, I stand above the Neva," 1868):

Лишь по задумчивой Неве
Струится лунное сиянье.

Only along the thoughtful Neva
The moon's radiance streams.

35. Haight, *Akhmatova*, p. 115.

36. Andrei Bely, *Petersburg*, translated, ann., and intro. Robert A. Maguire and John E. Malmstad (Bloomington: Indiana University Press, 1978), p. 13.

37. Dimitri M. Segal, "Fragment semanticheskoi poetiki O. E. Mandelstama" ("A Fragment of the Semantic Poetics of O. E. Mandelstam"), *Russian Literature* 10/11 (1975), p. 88.

38. Haight, *Akhmatova*, p. 154.

39. The contents of this material, located in Akhmatova's archive

in the Saltykov-Shchedrin Public Library in Leningrad, are described in Mandrykina, "Nenapisannaia kniga."

40. Ibid., p. 59.

41. Ibid., p. 61. Akhmatova's essay on postblockade Leningrad has been lost.

42. Ibid., p. 66.

43. See chapter 3, n. 6.

44. In the *Biblioteka poeta* edition (*Akhmatova: Stikhotvoreniia i poemy*) the word "mended" ("zashityi") appears in quotation marks, and "City" is capitalized: "Gorod."

45. As Filippov has observed: "*Poem Without a Hero* is a confession and a self-transformation for her in two senses, both religious and psychoanalytical: to remember, to resurrect all the circumstances of the distant past, like a stone lying on the soul, is to liberate oneself from something which oppresses and makes one's soul and spirit sink" (*Sochineniia*, 2:92).

46. *Akhmatova: Stikhotvoreniia i poemy*, p. 518.

The Second Petersburg: Conclusion

Like some of Dostoevsky's characters, Leningrad derives pride and almost a sensual pleasure from being "unrecognized," rejected; and yet, it's perfectly aware that, for everyone whose mother tongue is Russian, the city is more real than anywhere else in the world where this language is heard. For there is the second Petersburg, the one made of verses and of Russian prose.
    —Joseph Brodsky

Akhmatova, in her later years

*R*esiding in the "second Petersburg" from youth to old age, Akhmatova became one of its great modern architects. Her approach was both realistic and reverential: in creating a city habitable by Petersburgers of this century, she preserved the integrity of its original plan. From its almost imperceptible entrance into her poetry, in the aura of a white night or a glimpse of canal waters, Akhmatova's "second Petersburg" grew ever more insistent and imposing, coming at last to dominate her poetic landscape.

In making the city the stage of love's significant encounters, as did her Symbolist predecessors, she did not follow their example in seeking to transform it into a mystical decor, the domain of an elusive, unearthly Beloved or the gateway to another, more ideal realm of being. Nonetheless, her early city was a place of mystery and miracle: "Peter's miraculous city," with its shadows and strange plays of light, its miraculous air, its "moment of miracles" in the mysterious Summer Garden. In the emotional geography of her early poetry, Petersburg is the realm of intense, genuine, often terrifying emotion, looked back upon from the "safe," neutral afterlife of a country place.

Although Akhmatova is specific in her identification of city places, of time of day, of weather and season, the accuracy of her observations is subject to a transforming organizing principle: the sensibility of the lyrical heroine, for whom the city speaks, standing as objective correlative for complex inner states. This heroine is impervious to both the abuses and the allure of the city's new industrial technology. She does not hear the sounds of Blok's "booming city, wracked with trembling." Nor does she emerge from the sordid back entries of Dostoevsky's novels or make her way through the crowded, obscure streets of his Petersburg. Her arena is the majestic, classical city: its gardens, statues, monuments, cathedrals—and, above all, the Neva and its embankments.

She moves through this city with gratitude and delight, with fear, guilt, foreboding, and thinly concealed grief. At its brightest, it is the city whose delicate winter outline incarnates the "dark blessing" of her love affair, with its brief meetings and frequent partings. For, with a few, notable exceptions, which portray the lover's joyous arrival from the outside place to the inner precincts of the city, or a rare moment of fulfillment, these city poems speak overwhelmingly of love's failure. To the extent that a "reason" for this failure is given, it resides in the extraordinary, "unacceptable" nature of the heroine herself as poet, prophetess, witch. But the interest and achievement of these poems lie, not in their psychological dynamics alone, but in the merger of the heroine's situation with the image of the city.

The apocalyptic theme, associated with the city since Pushkin and given new impetus by the eschatological malaise besetting turn-of-the-century Russian artists and intellectuals, enters Akhmatova's Petersburg poetry in a personal, emotional key. The waters of the Neva, the city's eternal nemesis, become the focus of the heroine's anxiety, her sense of sin, guilt, and impending disaster. These evocations of Petersburg as "the sinful city"—Sodom, Babylon—or as a frozen realm, where the heroine is abandoned to her death, are among Akhmatova's darkest visions of the city. Yet even here she never generalizes her sense of love's dark fate to a principled rejection of Petersburg as the "accursed city" of anti-Petrine tradition. For "the sinful city" is still home, "native Sodom" as she calls it in "Lot's Wife," applying the adjective "rodnoi," which denotes both a formal and a spiritual kinship.

Akhmatova's conviction that one cannot "refuse to live one's own life" translates, in her poetry, into unqualified acceptance of the necessity, and privilege, of living in one's own city. If, like Pushkin, she is simultaneously aware of the city as a triumph of eternal form over fluctuating chaos, and as the embodiment of "the little man's" harsh fate, she is unique in embracing both meanings of the city's existence. In appropriating Petersburg as her spiritual birthplace, she describes its very darkness as nurturing ("The dark city on the terrible river was my blessed cradle"), the source of love, prayer, and poetry. Her sense of participation in the city's eternal life, as consolation for personal loss, is accompanied by sober recognition of the ominous, bounded stage of human endeavor: "above the dark-watered Neva, beneath the Emperor's cold smile." For Akhmatova, hardship, obstruction, are inseparable from the structure which lies at the root of beauty. Residence in "the splendid granite city of glory and misfortune," where life and death are inseparable and the voice of the Muse is overheard only at great cost, is a superior fate to "the simple life," Akhmatova's contrasting vision of easy, "normal" happiness.

When World War I and the Bolshevik Revolution brought an abrupt end to the old Petersburg life, the cataclysm was reflected in Akhmatova's city poetry, not in direct political or topical allusions, but in the generalized sense of a world in the throes of radical transformation, a city turned into "the opposite of itself," civilization returning to wilderness. ("The city of splendid military reviews has become like a wild camp.") Like Mandelstam, whose love of the city as a place of eternal forms and civilized rituals parallels her own, Akhmatova's sensibility was alien to that stream of thought, so widespread in prerevolutionary Russia, which welcomed the "coming Huns"[1] as a transfusion of primitive vitality into the anemic bloodstream of Europeanized Russia.

Petersburg's fall was for her an occasion, not of rejoicing, but of reaffirming an article of faith only half-articulated by her until then. The irrevocable loss of the old life was abruptly clear to her, but the City itself, as an ideal, spiritual reality, would survive. The uniqueness of Akhmatova's vision of Petersburg is never more apparent than in those poems of the immediately postrevolutionary years where she envisions its devastation, not as proof of the "accursed" barrenness of the city of the anti-Christ, but as a stage in the city's progress toward renewed grace. Her city of these years is a sinner-woman, bowed but possessed of infinite potential for repentance and salvation. The Russian Orthodox concept of salvation arising from the very depths of abasement and despair is reflected in her image of a long-awaited miracle approaching the outskirts of the devastated city. This is a vision of passive salvation, occurring without the necessity of human effort. But elsewhere Akhmatova perceived of the city's salvation in terms of the active intervention of its "fellow citizens," an elite "we" group, which chooses to defend the "palaces, fire and water" of "Peter's holy temple," which will henceforth stand as a monument to their sacrifice. In her vision of the defenders of the city, Akhmatova establishes a central tenet of her spiritual world: in order to preserve the eternal City, it is necessary to remain within the hellish city of the fixed historical moment.

A decade later, during the Terror, as it became increasingly difficult to perceive the outline of the ideal City behind the real one, this assertion of the sacred nature of participation in the national ordeal would take on an intensified, religious character. In her poetry of the 1930s, the city denied to the exiled prisoner became the prison of those left behind. Through the kindred figures of Dante and Mandelstam, she explored the essential duality of the lost native city of the exiled poet, "treacherous, base, long-awaited." In her perception of the invisible Soviet geography of those years, she placed Leningrad, not among the beautiful European capitals of the world, but at the center of the hellish network of Asian death camps. More terribly and absolutely than in the days of war and revolution, her city, "glorified by the first poet," had turned into the opposite of itself.

The degraded Leningrad of *Requiem* "hung like a useless pendant outside its prisons," impotent to provide either resistance to or spiritual refuge from the evils of the age. But Akhmatova returned the city to holy ground by making it, not a place of meaningless suffering, but Calvary. As she stands, three hundredth in line with her parcel, beneath the old Leningrad prison, "Crosses," she is Mary standing before the Cross. To the city she had designated her spiritual birthplace, she now bequeaths her own legacy: a bronze statue, to be placed on the spot where she waited in that prison line, an eternally grieving and remembering figure, embodying the "podvig": to be present at the place of Crucifixion. The city on the Neva stands under the aegis, not of Peter's cold, commanding figure, but of Mary's compassionate, sorrowful one. During the years of Leningrad's martyrdom, Akhmatova's poetry kept alive the image of an eternal home, a "blessed city" exempt from the trials of history. She resurrected the Russian legend of the drowned city of Kitezh, removed by the power of prayer to a timeless realm, to which the woman of Kitezh makes her way through "the crucified capital," past the atrocities and wars of the twentieth century. And in her poetry of Tashkent, she transformed the city which preserved her during the worst months of the blockade of Leningrad into her "Asian homeland," an exotic, sensually tangible, and intoxicating Kitezh.

The roads to Kitezh and Tashkent were, however, only brief detours from her path through the historical city. As Leningrad passed through the crucible of World War II, it was fully restored in her pantheon of values. She addressed the city's fragile treasures, its children, its statuary, with the bereaved, protective voice of a universal mother. As the city struggled against the foreign enemy, the "fellow citizens" of Akhmatova's earlier conception reappeared in the assertion of a continuous Leningrad community of the living and the dead, preservers of "the great Russian word." Akhmatova's phoenixlike Leningrad, rising from the ashes of war, would exist on two planes: a real city of saved children and victory parks and an ongoing cultural community, existing "outside of time."

In the graveyard of postwar Leningrad, she continued to mourn the enormity of the city's loss, to mark the "unforgettable, accursed dates" of her Leningrad calendar. The city as a place of inescapable disaster was an aspect of the Petersburg legend which had been actualized in Akhmatova's own life. Repeatedly, the furious waters of history had overrun their banks, carrying away beloved people, places, and things. The new kind of city poetry she created in her "historical landscape painting," replete with topical details of previous Petersburg eras, may be seen as an attempt to restore, within that "second Petersburg" of the literary imagination, the losses which had occurred in the first, historical city. Beyond the desire to recapture "lost time," however, she was also seeking a key to her generation's experience in an understanding of its "prehistory." And for this, she turned less to the historical city of the 1870s than to the "second," artistic city. Dostoevsky's pages, redolent of the place of execution, provide a link to the city of the Terror. Darkness, it would seem, is the portion of the city's heritage most easily passed on from generation to generation. But her attempt to garner a brighter inheritance, to perceive the city as a timeless community belonging to the artists who lived there and shaped its literary image, was frustrated by a sense of the mutual inaccessibility of distinct time periods. In the successive "Northern Elegies," time's implacable architecture overshadows the material city until Petersburg-Leningrad is nothing more than a changing name.

The temporal isolation revealed to her by her own unflinching artistic vision was compounded by a geographical isolation imposed by a government which denied her the right to foreign travel and penalized her heavily for contact with foreigners. If she was helpless to reverse time's edicts, she protested the harshness of her political fate by taking to the streets of her city and peopling them with shadows. The final stage of her Petersburg love poems, inspired by the 1946 meeting with Sir Isaiah Berlin, which played a role in her son's rearrest and her own literary denunciation, centers upon the notion of triumphant "nonmeetings." As in her early love poems, she introduces the motif of the lover who miraculously comes to her door. In the mortally weakened postwar city, he appears as a promise of new life; but this first meeting is also the last. Petersburg becomes the disembodied place of their subsequent nonmeetings. Another aspect of the Petersburg legend, the "spectral city," had been actualized in the circumstances of Akhmatova's life. For countless losses and deprivations had turned her city into a place where the shadow world possessed an equal—or greater—degree of reality for her than the material one. Amid the tangible beauties of the Summer Garden, she was pursued by a procession of shades. And in the streets of the city she continued to see its great, dead poets.

The outcome of her search for a poetic structure, which could encompass the full complexity of her vision of the city was *Poem without a Hero*, written and obsessively rewritten over the last quarter century of the poet's life. Akhmatova's masterpiece is as much about the second Petersburg as about the first, a grand resummoning, not only of the prerevolutionary Petersburg past, but of the city's literary tradition. Calling upon the image of that "fantastic Petersburg" which from Pushkin to Bely and Blok had been the very heart of the city's legend, she made of it an expression of the great themes of her later years: an implacable sense of guilt bound up with the past; the relentless epochs of memory and forgetting, which forever separate the living from the dead; and the contrasting vision of a spiritual victory over fate in the existence of an atemporal cultural community.

Taking its place alongside the delirium-wracked rooms of the city's dreamers, the author's room in the House on the Fontanka is transformed into a holy/unholy space, where living and dead may momentarily overcome their mutual isolation. In the masquerade of figures from the prerevolutionary era, which forms the *Poema*'s central "fantastic" event, the masques, in the tradition of Lermontov and Bely, whirl toward an inevitable hour of retribution, which is here both the Revolution which will put an end to their world and a Last Judgment, which still awaits. As the sinful night city of her youth, Petersburg-Sodom, rises before her, the author is tempted to flee; but her stronger impulse is to remain, to reunite her fate with that of her generation.

She achieves this through the nature of her characterizations, based upon the concept of "the double." Akhmatova does not employ this term, spawned in the delirium of the nineteenth-century city, in the Dostoevskian sense of a soul divided against itself. As she herself tells us, Sophocles, not Shakespeare, is her model. Through the double theme, enabling her to encounter herself in the figures of the past, she explores the interconnectedness of human fate. Olga Sudeykina, the Petersburg beauty, actress and femme fatale, for whom the young cornet takes his own life, is her most obvious double, one with whom she shares an unspoken guilt. But equally important are the images of other poets whose verses, like her own, are a part of the city's ongoing music: the poet as judge and lawmaker, dressed as a "striped milestone," which corresponds most closely to the figure of Mayakovsky; the divided half-demon, half-angel figure associated with Blok; and the Knyazev-Mandelstam figure, a composite image of the poet whose rival is the hostile age, and who sacrifices himself to the ideal of poetry.

Like the author, the city of the *Poema* views its image in a series of reflecting mirrors. It is Peter-Petersburg-Leningrad, the malleable, continually shifting medium, through which Akhmatova expresses her sense of human history. Through its center runs the Lethe-Neva, a river which appeared in an elegiac poem of 1940, to express her sense of a lost Petersburg world, and which occurs at the outset of Andrey Bely's great novel, *Petersburg*. As in Bely, the *Poema's* vision of the city between this world and the next expresses the instability and chaotic nature of a culture on the verge of destruction. The notion of approaching doom permeates Akhmatova's spectral city. An encompassing image of retribution, it is both Pursued and Pursuer; the seething, external wintry world, threatening to engulf the internal world of art; the barren city cursed by Tsaritsa Avdotya; a "Dostoevskian and possessed" apocalyptic landscape. Yet in this, her most developed evocation of "the accursed city," culminating in the approach, along the legendary quay, of "not the calendar, but the True Twentieth Century," Akhmatova is summarizing the tradition of Petersburg's apocalyptic poems and is giving it the conclusion dictated by her own deep perspective; she is not writing a true "Poem of the End." The "accursed city" is not her final word on Petersburg.

For in the "Epilogue" to the *Poema*, the outlines of a philosophy of history, reconciling the accursed city with the blessed one, may be discerned: a vision of the city as a many-layered temporal structure, whose separate levels are united by an indestructible internal essence. The juxtaposition of city/years provides a medium for discovery of the city's eternal nature. Stress shifts from 1913 as a single, irreversible cataclysm, to 1942, a year of the siege, as part of the city's cyclical deaths and resurrections. The notions of recovery and survival are closely bound up with the author herself, as one who has repeatedly survived the disasters of both Love and History. If, in her youth, belonging to the city assured the "immortality" of a failed love affair, now what is foremost is the inseparability of the poet and the city, within whose precincts she has lived out her destiny. In her final vindication of the city, she defines its wholeness as a feature of its continual struggle to survive the devastations of successive eras, and to wrest from that struggle a human word.

In the Pushkinian legend, "history," represented by the building of the city upon the Finnish marshes, contains the insoluble paradox: beauty, form, the creation of human values achieved at the expense of "the little man." Nature symbolizes chaos, continually threatening to reclaim what cosmos has won, as well as the forces of hubris, punishing man for overstepping his natural bounds. For Akhmatova, there are two histories: the True Twentieth Century of world wars and concentration camps—the mindless chaos in which no positive value redeems the loss of individual lives; and the positive transformation of this chaos within the history of art, perceived as an ongoing community of creators of beauty and human values. The city represents the permanent intertwinement of these two histories. In its harmony of natural and architectural elements, it forms a vast "seashell" through which the winds of world history blow. The sound of this seashell may be the "rumble" of revolution, the howling of an old woman outside the prison, the unearthly deathsound of the first aerial bombardment. Yet even in these incursions, chaos is contained, subordinated to "the music of the marvelous meter of the wild Leningrad wind."

Akhmatova's final legacy to her city was thus greater than the monument she designed for herself in *Requiem*. Inheriting the tormented Petersburg myth of the nineteenth century, and given ample opportunity to affirm its dark message, she nonetheless transformed Petersburg-Leningrad into a triumphant metaphor of survival. In the final analysis, the source of the faith illuminating and redeeming her unsparing vision of the True Twentieth-Century City is as mysterious as Petersburg's astounding light:

> И все перламутром и яшмой горит,
> Но света источник таинственно скрыт.

> *And everything burns like mother-of-pearl and jasper,*
> *But the source of the light is mysteriously hidden.*

Notes

1. "Griadushchie Gunny" ("The Coming Huns") is a famous poem by Valery Bryusov which welcomes the barbarian invaders and exults in the destruction of culture.

Selected Bibliography

1. Works by Anna Akhmatova

For a listing of works by Akhmatova published prior to 1976, the reader is referred to Amanda Haight, *Anna Akhmatova: A Poetic Pilgrimage* (New York and London: Oxford University Press, 1976), p. 199. The single most complete edition of Akhmatova's works is *Sochineniia* (*Works*), vol. 1, 2d ed., vol. 2, ed. G. P. Struve and B. A. Filippov, (Munich and Washington, D.C.: Inter-Language Literary Associates, 1967–68). Posthumous collections not listed by Haight or published in or after 1976 include:

Izbrannoe (*Selected Works*). Moscow, 1974.

Stikhi i proza (*Poems and Prose*). Leningrad, 1976.

Stikhotvoreniia i poemy (*Selected Works*). Compiled by V. M. Zhirmunsky. Biblioteka poeta. Leningrad, 1976.

Stikhotvoreniia (*Selected Works*). Compiled by N. Bannikov. Moscow, 1977.

Anna Akhmatova: Stikhi/Perepiska/Vospominaniia/Ikonografiia (*Anna Akhmatova: Poems/Correspondence/Reminiscences/Iconography*). Compiled by E. Proffer. Ann Arbor: Ardis, 1977.

Anna Akhmatova o Pushkine (*Anna Akhmatova on Pushkin*). With an afterword by Emma Gershtein. Leningrad, 1977.

2. Other Works

The following list includes the major sources quoted in this work, as well as other works consulted for background information but not quoted directly.

Afanasev, K. A., Zakharov, V. V., and Tomashevsky, B. V., comps. *Peterburg, Petrograd, Leningrad v russkoi poezii (Petersburg, Petrograd, Leningrad in Russian Poetry).* Leningrad, 1975.

Antsiferov, Nikolay Pavlovich. *Dusha Peterburga (The Soul of Petersburg).* Petersburg, 1922.

———. *Byl' i mif Peterburga (Fact and Myth of Petersburg).* Petersburg, 1924.

———. *Prigorody Leningrada (Suburbs of Leningrad).* Moscow, 1946.

Belinsky, Vissarion. "Peterburg i Moskva" ("Petersburg and Moscow"). In *Sobranie sochinenii v trëkh tomakh (Collected Works in Three Volumes),* vol. 2. Moscow, 1948.

Bely, Andrei. *Petersburg.* Translated, annotated, and introduced by Robert A. Maguire and John E. Malmstad. Bloomington and London: Indiana University Press, 1978.

Berlin, Isaiah. *Personal Impressions.* London: Hogarth Press, 1980.

Blok, Alexander. *Sobranie sochinenii (Collected Works).* Moscow and Leningrad, 1960.

Brodsky, Joseph. "Leningrad: A Great Poet's Guide to a City of Mystery." *Vogue,* September 1979, pp. 494–547.

Brown, Clarence. *The Prose of Osip Mandelstam.* Princeton: Princeton University Press, 1965.

Bryusov, Valery. *Stikhotvoreniia i poemy (Selected Works).* Leningrad, 1960.

Chukovskaya, Lydia. *Zapiski ob Anne Akhmatovoi (Notes about Anna Akhmatova).* 2 vols. Paris: YMCA Press, 1976–80.

Chukovsky, Korney. "Anna Akhmatova." In *Sobranie sochinenii (Collected Works).* Moscow, 1967.

———. *Ot Chekhova do nashikh dnei (From Chekhov until Our Times).* Petersburg, 1908. Reprint ed. Ann Arbor: University Microfilms, 1968.

Dobin, E. *Poeziia Anny Akhmatovoi (The Poetry of Anna Akhmatova).* Leningrad, 1968.

Dolgopolov, L. K. "Po zakonam pritiazheniia" ("By the Laws of Attraction"). *Russkaia literatura,* no. 4 (1979), pp. 38–58.

Donchin, Georgette. *The Influence of French Symbolism on Russian Poetry.* The Hague: Mouton, 1958.

Driver, Sam. *Anna Akhmatova.* New York: Twayne, 1972.

Eikhenbaum, Boris. *Anna Akhmatova.* Petrograd, 1923.

Eliot, T. S. *Selected Essays.* London: Faber and Faber, 1951.

Erlich, Victor. *The Double Image*. Baltimore: Johns Hopkins University Press, 1964.

Fanger, Donald. *Dostoevsky and Russian Romanticism*. Cambridge, Mass.: Harvard University Press, 1965.

Fedotov, George P. *The Russian Religious Mind*. New York: Harper, 1946.

Filippov, Boris. "Poema bez geroia." In Anna Akhmatova, *Sochineniia*, vol. 2. Washington, D.C.: Inter-Language Literary Associates, 1968.

————. *Leningradskii Peterburg v russkoi poezii i proze* (*Leningrad-Petersburg in Russian Poetry and Prose*). Paris: La Press Libre, 1974.

Frank, Victor. "Beg vremeni." In Anna Akhmatova, *Sochineniia*, vol. 2. Washington, D.C.: Inter-Language Literary Associates, 1968.

Gogol, Nikolay. *Sochineniia v dvukh tomakh* (*Collected Works in Two Volumes*). Moscow, 1975.

Haight, Amanda. *Anna Akhmatova: A Poetic Pilgrimage*. New York and London: Oxford University Press, 1976.

Herzen, A. I. "Moskva i Peterburg" ("Moscow and Petersburg"). In *Sobranie sochinenii* (*Collected Works*), vol. 2. Moscow, 1934.

Ivanov, Evgeny. "Vsadnik: nechto o gorode Peterburge" ("The Horseman: Something on the City of Petersburg"). In *Belye nochi*, vol. 1. Petersburg, 1907.

Ivask, George. "The Vital Ambivalence of Petersburg." *Texas Studies in Literature and Language* 17 (1975), pp. 247–55.

Koubourlis, Demetrius J. *A Concordance to the Poems of Osip Mandelstam*. Ithaca: Cornell University Press, 1974.

Lermontov, M. Y. *Sobranie sochinenii v chetyrëkh tomakh* (*Collected Works in Four Volumes*). Moscow and Leningrad, 1962.

Mandelstam, Nadezhda. *Hope against Hope*. New York: Atheneum, 1970.

————. *Hope Abandoned*. New York: Atheneum, 1974.

Mandelstam, Osip. *Sobranie sochinenii v trëkh tomakh* (*Collected Works in Three Volumes*). Edited by G. P. Struve and B. A. Filippov. Washington, D.C.: Inter-Language Literary Associates, 1964–71.

Mandrykina, L. A. "Nenapisannaia kniga: Listki iz dnevnika A. A. Akhmatovoi" ("An Unfinished Book: Pages from a Diary of

Anna Akhmatova"). In *Knigi, arkhivy, avtografy* (*Books, Archives, Autographs*). Moscow, 1973.

Mumford, Lewis. *The City in History*, New York: Harcourt, Brace and World, 1961.

Murray, Henry A. "Introduction to the Issue: Myth and Mythology," *Daedalus*, spring 1959, pp. 211–22.

Pamiati A. Akhmatovoi (*In Memory of A. Akhmatova*). Paris: YMCA Press, 1974.

Pavlovsky, A. I. *Anna Akhmatova*. Leningrad, 1966.

Pipes, Richard, trans. and ed. *Karamzin's Memoir on Ancient and Modern Russia*. New York: Atheneum, 1966.

Proffer, Carl R. "*A Poem without a Hero*: Notes and Commentary." In *A Poem without a Hero*, trans. C. R. Proffer and A. Humesky. Ann Arbor: Ardis, 1973.

Pushkin, Alexander. *Polnoe sobranie sochinenii* (*Complete Collected Works*). Moscow, 1964.

Rannit, Alexis. "Anna Akhmatova Considered in a Context of Art Nouveau." In Anna Akhmatova, *Sochineniia*, vol. 2. Washington, D.C.: Inter-Language Literary Associates, 1968.

Rude, Jeanne. *Anna Akhmatova*. Paris: P. Seghers, 1968.

Segal, D. M. "Fragment semanticheskoi poetiki O. E. Mandelstama" ("A Fragment of the Semantic Poetics of O. E. Mandelstam"). *Russian Literature* 10/11 (1975), pp. 59–146.

Shklovsky, Victor. *Za i protiv: Zametki o Dostoevskom* (*Pro and Contra: Remarks on Dostoevsky*). Moscow, 1957.

Stewart, T. C. *The City as an Image of Man*. London: Latimer Press, 1970.

Timenchik, R. *Materialy XXII nauchnoi studencheskoi konferentsii* (*Materials of the Twenty-Second Academic Student Conference*). Tartu, 1967.

Tomashevsky, B. V., ed. *Pushkinskii Peterburg* (*Pushkin's Petersburg*). Leningrad, 1949.

Van der Eng-Liedmeier, Jeanne. "Poema bez geroia." In *Tale without a Hero and Twenty-Two Poems by Anna Akhmatova*, ed. J. Van der Eng-Liedmeier and K. Verheul. The Hague: Mouton, 1973.

Verheul, Kees. *The Theme of Time in the Poetry of Anna Akhmatova*. The Hague and Paris: Mouton, 1971.

———. "Public Themes in the Poetry of Anna Akhmatova." In *Tale without a Hero and Twenty-Two Poems by Anna Akhmatova*, ed. J.

Van der Eng-Liedmeier and K. Verheul. The Hague: Mouton, 1973.

Vinogradov, V. *O poezii Anny Akhmatovoi* (*On The Poetry of Anna Akhmatova*). Leningrad, 1925.

Weimar, David R. *The City as Metaphor*. New York: Random House, 1966.

Zhirmunsky, V. M. "Preodolevshie Simvolizm" ("Those Who Overcame Symbolism"). *Russkaia mysl'* 12 (1916), part 2, pp. 32–41.

———. "Anna Akhmatova i Alexander Blok," *Russkaia literatura*, no. 3 (1970), pp. 57–82.

———. *Tvorchestvo Anny Akhmatovoi* (*The Work of Anna Akhmatova*). Leningrad, 1973.

Index of Names and Subjects

Index of Poems by Akhmatova